RIDE ALONG WITH

Dale Earnhardt Jr.
2005

PRECISION
PUBLISHING

This book is available in quantity at special discounts for your group or organization. For further information, contact:

Precision Publishing
1515 Mockingbird Lane, Suite 803
Charlotte, North Carolina 28209
(704) 525-4513
(704) 525-8946

Design By:

NASCAR Publishing
Senior Manager of Publishing - Jennifer White
Publishing Coordinator - Catherine McNeill

Copywriter - Holly Cain

CORNERSTONE
D E S I G N

Cornerstone Design, Inc.
Berea, KY
(859) 986-8776

Printed in the USA
ISBN 0-9758854-3-X

All photographs courtesy of Autostock Images

Acknowledgements

If it is true that adversity builds character, Dale Earnhardt Jr. should have enough to last a lifetime. Every driver experiences just such a season, the great ones bounce back and resume there visits to victory lane. Earnhardt's late season charge fell short of securing a spot in the Top 10, but there is no doubt in anyone's mind that Earnhardt and DEI have their eyes focused on 2006. Despite having a season that he'd like to forget, Earnhardt's fans have continued there unwavering support. Ride Along With Dale Earnhardt Jr. 2005 is for those fans who are loyal through good and bad.

Precision Publishing would like to thank all the people involved in the production of this year's edition. First, thanks go out to NASCAR; including Mark Dyer, Jennifer White, Catherine McNeill and Liz Schlosser.

The photography in this book was provided by Cameras In Action. Precision extends a special thanks to everyone at CIA including, Erine Masche, Don Grassman, Mike Simmons, Gary Eller, Tom Copeland, and Angie Patterson for all their dedication to this project.

Greer Smith undertook the difficult task of writing the account of this season. Thanks for a job well done goes out to Greer for his attention to detail and his guidance.

Presenting the pages that follow was the work of Mr. Duane Knight at Cornerstone Design. Duane continues to outdo himself making each book look even better than the last.

Please Enjoy
Charlie Keiger
President
Precision Publishing

Table of Contents

Despite a disappointing year on the track in 2005, Dale Earnhardt Jr. still remained first in one area.

Popularity.

He still remained No. 1 in the hearts of his fans.

He still remained swamped with requests from companies asking for endorsement of their products, finally deciding to put his stamp on an energy chewing gum called XLR8. He continued with his Jr. Motorsports development program, deciding to put Mark McFarland in the NASCAR Busch Series with backing from the Navy.

While his performances in the Budweiser Chevrolet weren't up to expectations, the fans still came to autograph sessions in droves. Even though he struggled to run in the top 10 at times, they flocked to the music concerts that he hosted.

More cars streaming into the parking lots at race tracks carried No.8 stickers and decals and flags than the numbers and flags of any other driver.

They continued to express their loyalty by keeping Earnhardt first in voting for NASCAR's most popular driver award. They continue to post words of encouragement on the Internet.

He felt their pain and disappointment in addition to his over the failure at not making the Chase for the NASCAR NEXTEL Cup and his mediocre runs at a number of races. He felt their frustration in addition to his over the swap of cars and crews between Earnhardt and Michael Waltrip ending in failure.

He recognized the importance of their support and backing that he made a promise to them when he was officially eliminated from the Chase for the NASCAR NEXTEL Cup on one of his most disappointing night of the season.

After his engine failed spectacularly by sending a stream of smoke trailing from the Budweiser Chevrolet, Earnhardt assured the faithful that thing would be better next year.

"I promise that we will be back in victory lane," he said.

And his DEI team quickly made changes to make that happen by reversing a preseason move and returned Tony Eury Jr. to Earnhardt's crew.

Judging by the improvement in Earnhardt's performance over the final 10 races with Tony Jr. as crew chief , he appears well on the way to making good on his pledge.

Even though he was stymied by wrecks in a four-race stretch at Talladega, Kansas City, Charlotte and Martinsville, Earnhardt demonstrated he had a car capable of running in the top ten every week.

He gave an indication of the team's potential by leading 142 laps on the way to finish fourth at Atlanta and backed that up with a strong run at Texas.

All of it points to a return to the success of 2004, when Earnhardt won six races. All of it points to a berth in the chase and another run to the championship in 2006.

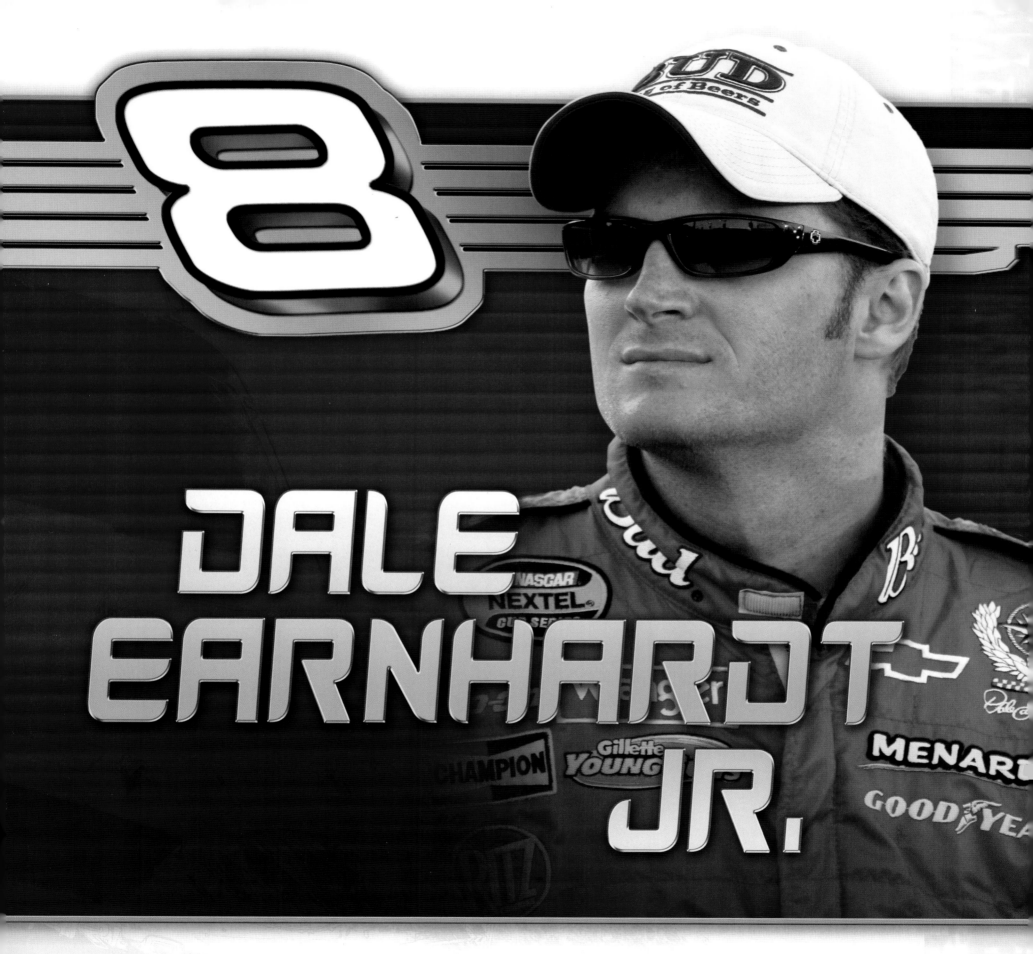

Daytona Speedweeks to Martinsville

Plenty of questions marks swirled around Dale Earnhardt Jr. and his team as they prepared for Daytona Speedweeks and the start of the 2005 season.

How long would it take Earnhardt to get accustomed to his new cars and crew as a result of the swap with teammate Michael Waltrip? Could the DEI combo remain as the dominant drivers in restrictor plate racing at Daytona and Talladega? After leaving Daytona, how well would the team would adapt to NASCAR's new aerodynamics package featuring a shorter rear spoiler designed to produce less downforce combined with tires having a softer rubber compound.?

One cloud not hanging over his head was the lack of a Daytona 500 victory. Instead, he felt relaxed as the defending champion of the race that he coveted the most.

"Well, it's pretty cool to come in here and not have to worry about it," Earnhardt said during January testing. "It's a great track, great area and there are awesome restaurants. And I can take all that stuff in now. It would be awesome to win it again but that first one--it's almost a nag to try to win it and all the frustration that goes into it. It's tough to lose it but to finally get it out of the way and be able to take it lap-for-lap is good. I don't have to get an ulcer over the first 499 miles and wait on that last lap. Now we can just race."

The concern once Speedweeks began was how stout Earnhardt and Waltrip were compared to years past and if Jeff Gordon and his Hendrick Motorsports team, winners of two restrictor plate events in 2004, had become the equal of DEI.

Speculation that DEI had slipped began when both Earnhardt and Waltrip were off the pace in January testing and in opening practice for Daytona 500 qualifying.

The chatter that DEI was no longer invincible picked up when Earnhardt finished seventh in the Budweiser Shootout featuring 2004 pole winners.

Earnhardt started in the rear of the 20-car field following a transmission change and an electrical problem kept him there during the 70-lap event's first segment. Earnhardt said his engine began misfiring from the start and during the intermission his crew changed ignition modules and installed a new set of spark plug wires.

The changes worked. Earnhardt started the second segment in 18th and peaked out when he reached fourth place on lap 31. Battling a loose car, he was unable to break out of the back and gained three spots on the final lap to come away with seventh place.

"The car was a bit loose there, but it was fun," he said. "We needed more time. I got up toward the front and then got shuffled back. The last couple of laps we were moving back up there."

The next day, the prospects for a repeat win in the Daytona 500 looked pretty dim when Earnhardt qualified 39th and Waltrip was just six spots better.

"It's hard to do it by myself," he said. "We're way, way down on horsepower. And that's just the simple fact of it.

"We've been real slow since we've been here. We were slow in the test. So our expectations have been pretty low as far as qualifying. We picked up a little bit so that made the team happy. We picked up about a tenth. But we didn't expect to be real high on the board."

Fortunately, the qualifying only decided starting positions for the Daytona's unique twin 150-mile qualifying races. Earnhardt predicted that the DEI cars would run well in the draft to compensate for the lack of horsepower.

"The car races really well in the draft. If everything works fine, we'll have a good race on Thursday and get up front sooner or later. But, to run by ourselves, we need more steam underneath the hood. I've kind of seen it coming and the test wasn't that good."

He was prediction about the qualifying race was right on the money. He and Waltrip worked through the pack early in the 60-lap even and Waltrip blasted into the lead on lap 33.

Pit stops in a caution period left Johnny Sauter in front on lap 45. Mike Skinner moved into the top spot on lap 51 and was still there on the final restart with four laps to go.

Earnhardt, who fought a loose car earlier, took the lead from Skinner with a push from Waltrip just after they took the white flag.

Coming out of turn four, Waltrip squeezed to the inside of Earnhardt and used enough side drafting to edge ahead at the finish line.

"He pushed me into the lead and I thought I might be able to hold onto it, but he got a run," Earnhardt said. It was the last corner on the last lap and I wasn't about to throw a block on him in a qualifying race."

Despite the run that gave him fifth starting position in the 500, Earnhardt said his car needed improvement.

"About mid-way through the race I was fighting a handling issue. My car was really loose. We put tires on it and adjusted it a little bit. We've got to work on it some more. We fought it real bad in the test in race trim this car is really loose. It showed up again today in the middle of the race. Other than that, it was pretty cool."

The handling trouble cropped up again in the 500, but this time the Budweiser Chevrolet was too tight. Earnhardt ran in midpack for 150 laps before he was able muster a charge down the stretch of an event that went three laps past its scheduled 200-lap distance.

Sitting 17th on a lap 173 restart, he was fifth by the time the yellow flag waved on lap 184, the first of three yellows in the last 18 laps.

Sitting third on a lap 195 restart, Earnhardt passed Tony Stewart and Jeff Gordon to take the lead for the first time. Stewart led lap 196

and Earnhardt managed to lead lap 197 before Gordon shot past both of them. Earnhardt finished third.

"I was really surprised because that we were position to win with 15 laps to go," Earnhardt said. "I'm telling you, man, the car was way, way off at one point. We were running pretty good there, just kind of beating and banging around in there in the middle about 10th. It was hard. There were guys going three wide a lot. My car was really good, if I could get up against the wall, and I could really make runs off the corner. But every time I did that, the guy behind me would try to go to the middle and screw it all up.

"We just kept doing that all day long, I wasn't getting anywhere. I couldn't ever get to the front. I wasn't even close to the front. We put on a set of tires in the middle of the race and then the car just drove like it had a big hole in the nose. It wouldn't turn and pushed real bad. I was having to lift way, way early getting down in the corner and it just pushed to the wall, I'd have to run about half throttle. We barely hung onto the draft there at the end during that whole deal.

"We had two more pit stops. I told him, Man, you got to do a lot of stuff to get this thing freed up. They did. They did exactly what I needed them to. That was one of the best cars out there at the end of the race."

Earnhardt said he was powerless to mount a defense when Gordon drove by on the outside coming off turn two to take the lead for the final time.

"I saw Gordon kind of getting a run, so I pulled up in front of him as best I could. We went down into turn one and I went to the bottom. He kind of stayed to the outside. I couldn't tell whether I had him perfectly cleared or not. I didn't move up in front of him. I didn't want to get up in front of him and have him jack me up or anything like that. I still thought by the exit of the corner I might be able to have him still cleared and be able to put my car in front of him then. He had such a run, and I was by myself. He was going by so fast, I couldn't even draft off the side of his car, slow him down. He was gone. I was just fortunate. I was feeling real

lucky just to be in second at that point because I could have lost a couple more spots there."

The week marked the first time in four years that Earnhardt failed to win during Speedweeks.

"I got third in the Busch race and second in the 150. So that's two seconds and a third and that's not bad. I know I can't win them all but I still like to keep my average high."

Leaving Daytona, the team faced its firs big test of the year the next week in the first February race at California Speedway.

In addition to being a track where Earnhardt had struggled in the past, it was the first race for the aerodynamic package with a 4-inch rear spoiler, a full inch shorter than in 2004.

The weekend got off on the wrong foot when Earnhardt qualified 40th for the 500-mile event, which he attributed to a mistake on his part.

"We had a great car and it looked like we were going to work ourselves up there," Earnhardt said. "I thought we had a top 10 car at the start of that race and we got it even better."

He climbed into the top 25 by the 30th lap. Six laps later, he suffered a flat left-front tire, resulting in a green flag pit stop that put him a lap down. Just 22 laps later, he suffered the same problem again but with far more serious consequences.

The tire shredded and ripped away the left-front fender before Earnhardt could make it to the pits.

"The tires just kept going flat," Earnhardt said. "You'll have to talk to Pete and those guys about what they think the initial cause was, but the car was handling great.

"I was really proud of the way the car drove. And even after we fixed all the problems and didn't have any more flats, it was still driving alright. I just didn't want to get up there and racing those guys that were on the lead lap."

Earnhardt said he unsure why he did not have any more trouble. He wound up finishing 33rd, 17 laps behind winner Greg Biffle.

"You know, those tires going flat — that was weird," Earnhardt said. "We didn't change anything and we didn't have any problems any

more. We didn't change. We stayed at the air pressures — everything was the same. They just quit, blowing out."

He said the short spoiler did nothing to help produce side-by-side racing, one of the reasons NASCAR instituted the change.

"I don't think that makes any sense to take that much off the spoiler and say it's going to make it better running side-by-side, obviously," he said. "Somebody's got to wake up here, you know what I mean? They've got to figure this out. Taking the spoiler off it is going to make it more difficult to drive.

"I'd like to get an inch of spoiler back. Give me an inch more spoiler and give me some more front downforce. Give us all that, you know, give us everything. Then we'll have a hell of a race, you know what I mean?. The cars don't turn, and they don't grip in the back too good. I don't want to complain too much because I got my car driving pretty good, comparable to everybody else, you know what I mean? Everybody was just all over the place coming off the corners. But, I think if they give us a lot of downforce, you know, we could race a lot closer and charge the corner, get on the outside of guys. When you don't have that spoiler on there, if you get to the outside and it shows the nose on that air, shoot man, it just spins out."

He had little opportunity to make progress with the smaller spoiler the next week at Las Vegas.

Just 12 laps into the 400-mile event, Earnhardt ran into the rear of Brian Vickers entering turn one. Vickers spun and slammed into Earnhardt, who trying to get past on the outside. Both were sidelined, with Earnhardt getting 42nd place and dropping all the way to 27th in points.

The wreck occurred moments after Earnhardt let Vickers go by.

"That was a big mistake on my part," Earnhardt said. "I went into the corner like I though I should, and he went in there a little easier than I expected. I ran all over him. It was my fault and I apologized to him."

After two rough outings, Atlanta Motor Speedway offered a chance for a rebound as Earnhardt tried to defend his win in the 2004 Golden Corral 500. But, a loose race car and two penalties for speeding on pit road put the brakes on a rally.

The penalties left Earnhardt two laps behind and he was still at that deficit at the end in a 24th-place finish.

"We were really loose most of the day and at times the car was hard to drive," Earnhardt said. "But we had a car that could have finished a lot better than it did, and that was my fault. I was too fast exiting pit road. We fell two laps down and we could never recover.
"I can't knock anybody but myself. I knew when it happened, I was going too fast. I feel pretty bad about it."

Earnhardt finally got a chance to take advantage of the misfortunes of others in gutting out a fourth-place finish at Bristol in the Food City 500.

Although not as potent as in his win last August at the .533-mile bullring, he was able to stay in the top 10 over the last 400 laps. Although he did not lead, he dodged the crashes and tire troubles that befell many. The second top-five finish of the season boosted Earnhardt to 17th in points.

"We had a lot better car with 100 laps to go. We made some adjustments and it started sliding around a little, but we held on for a top five. We had a real good car in the middle of the race and I was happy with how the team got through the day."

He wasn't as fortunate at Martinsville. He sustained fender damage when a number of cars jammed together on the first lap of the 500-lap event. Later, he spun on lap 285 and then sustained fender damage in two more incidents, one of them a collision with Mike Bliss.

He picked up one spot following a restart with three laps remaining and finished 13th, good enough to advance a spot in points to 16th.

"That was one of the craziest races I've ever been in," Earnhardt said. "We had all kinds of problems, but we made a decent day out of it. It would have been nice to finish in the top 10, but I'm happy to come out of here with a car in one piece."

TEXAS TO NASCAR NEXTEL ALL-STAR CHALLENGE

Bolstered by the fourth place at Bristol, Dale Earnhardt Jr. headed into a stretch of six races that would give an indication of how well the crew swap was working and how much progress it had made adjusting to the new aerodynamic package.

The swing running from Texas Motor Speedway through the all-star race included five places where he had won before (Texas, Phoenix International Raceway, Talladega Superspeedway, Richmond International Raceway and the all-star event at Lowe's Motor Speedway). The only exception was Darlington Raceway, where his best previous finish was fourth in 2002.

And it began with promise. Soon after the Samsung/Radio Shack 500 began, Earnhardt had the form that helped produce his first Cup victory in 2000 at the 1.5-mile Texas track. Starting 11th, he surged into the top five by the 50-lap mark in the 334-lap event.

He remained in the top ten early, struggled in the middle section the surged again and climbed into the top five before making his final pit stop under caution with just over 30 laps to go.

After the green flag waved for the final time, Earnhardt faded and wound up with a disappointing ninth-place finish.

After the race he was critical of Goodyear's tires and of the shorter rear spoiler in the new aerodynamic package.

"It was a frustrating way to end it," Earnhardt said. "I thought we had a top-five car at the end. We were getting stronger and stronger, and then we put on the last of tires and it just got too tight. It is just frustrating that you work that hard, work into having a top-five car, and than have a set of tires be off that much.

Earnhardt said his car felt like it was going to spin on every lap. On the day, six wrecks helped lead to 11 yellow flag periods that slowed 56 laps.

Some of the drivers involved blamed the wrecks on the reduction of downforce brought by the shorter spoilers.

The shorter spoiler is part of a package that NASCAR officials hoped would lessen the importance of aerodynamics, and to reduced the amount of aerodynamic push that one car encounters when it rides behind another car. Drivers blamed aerodynamic push, or the tendency of a car not to turn when behind another car, as the reason that passing is difficult at all but the short tracks and road courses.

"The aero push has been around since the second car ever built drove behind the first one ever built. You're not going to get rid of that, no matter what you do. They got the aero push just as bad as when they had no spoiler on it, so I don't know why they wouldn't put it back on."

Earnhardt said the race was another example of the team starting to pick up the pace following an adjustment period in the wake of the crew swap.

"I've stepped up my commitment. I started out the year relaxed, and allowing those guys to get used to the change first. With me coming in there I didn't really want to push them hard at the start. But, we're starting to get into the season. Me and Pete (Rondeau, crew chief), we're starting to work a little harder and demand a little more from ourselves around the race track. We're driving real, real hard to get good finishes for this team and keep them going."

He continued driving hard the next week trying to pick up his third straight victory at Phoenix in the first spring race and the first night race at that track.

In pursuit of another win on the flat mile track, Earnhardt had to deal with one big disadvantage. He was not able to drive the car that he used in winning the previous two events. That one went to

Waltrip in the team swap, leaving Earnhardt to get accustomed to Waltrip's former equipment.

In the early stages, he realized he was trying too hard to work his way to the front from 15th starting position in the 312-lap event.

"I started to run it deep into the corners in the first 50 laps and the car wasn't working," Earnhardt said. "I just stepped back and slowed down a little bit. Man, that's when it started working and I started passing people."

After bouncing around the top ten for most of the night, a decision not to pit during a late caution gave Earnhardt the track position he needed to finish fourth, two spots behind Waltrip in the best effort to that point of the season for DEI.

"I just can't believe how hard of work it is," Earnhardt said. "Things have become a lot easier, but man, we're all working really, really hard. There ain't nobody in that shop that ain't putting forth the hardest effort. It's amazing. Sometimes, you know, when you don't get those finishes like we got tonight, it's real disappointing. It just feels good to get a good finish."

A good finish was more than Earnhardt expected the next week at Talladega, a track where he had won five of the previous six races. The main question surrounding the entire weekend was if Earnhardt would regain his dominance in restrictor-plate racing from Jeff Gordon, who came into the weekend with wins in three of the four previous restrictor plate races at Daytona and Talladega?

As at Daytona, Earnhardt was off the mark in qualifying and landed in 36th starting position for the Aaron's Rents 499. Just as at Daytona, he was confident that he could work his way into contention through his prowess in working the draft.

He didn't disappoint and eventually moved into the lead by gunning past Kevin Harvick on lap 89 of the 192-lap contest. But, he was not as powerful as in the past and stayed there for only three laps in his only time at the front as 16 drivers traded the lead 33 times.

"People will push you to the front if you are fast and they get tired of pushing you if you are slow," Earnhardt said. "That was it. We were slow."

He stayed near the front and was eventually involved in two wrecks. He escaped damage in the first crash, a 25-car pileup on lap 133 that started

when Jimmie Johnson bumped Mike Wallace as they raced three abreast with Scott Riggs. A fraction of a second after Johnson squeezed Wallace into Riggs, Earnhardt hit Wallace from behind.

"(Johnson) ran (Wallace) into (Riggs) and the fence," Earnhardt said. "I was pushing (Wallace) and the guy beside him, who I was told was (Johnson), squeezed him into (Riggs) and they all hit the fence.

Earnhardt managed to stay in the lead draft until he was bumped by Johnson on the backstretch on lap 187. Earnhardt bounced off a wall and spun as the cars of his teammate Martin Truex Jr., Greg Biffle, Harvick and Travis Kvapil became involved.

I was going straight and then into the wall," Earnhardt said. "I'm not sure what happened beside me there. I came up the track a little bit, but I didn't think that I come up a lot. But I must have squeezed somebody up into the wall or something.

After some hasty repairs, Earnhardt limped to a 15th-place finish. He said his car was his worst here since his rookie season in 2000.

"Nothing's wrong, but we just aren't the best here anymore," he said. "We're good, but not the best and we used to be the best."

He suffered again in qualifying at Darlington, winding up in 39th starting position. But, thanks to some chassis adjustments and quick pick work, he came away with an eighth place in the Charger 500 to finish in the top ten for the fourth time in six races.

He advanced to the top 15 by lap 53 and barged into the top ten on lap 82 of an event that stretched to 370 laps in a green-white-checkered overtime finish. He moved from 10th to eighth in pit stops on lap 317 and he managed to hang on to that position at the end of the first night race at the narrow 1.366-mile track that held its first Cup race in 1950.

"I had fun, about as much as you can have at this old place," Earnhardt said. "We worked really hard to get that finish. We had great pit stops all night and a great engine.

"I've been complaining about the engines. But, the whole company is working hard and we are seeing results on the track. We had a

terrible qualifying lap and a long way to go. So, it feels good to finish as high as we did."

Earnhardt had country music star Jo Dee Messina in his pits the next week for the Chevy American Revolution 400 at Richmond, but she failed to bring him a lot of luck. Earnhardt appeared in the early stages of the 400-lap event that he may have a car capable of winning as he charged from 27th starting position to gain 10 spots in the early laps.

But, his progress stalled and he then suffered a set back when he was caught speeding on pit road during caution on lap 128 and had to restart at the rear of the field on lap 133.

"When the race started, I thought we were going to be great because we were passing cars pretty easy," Earnhardt said. "Then the car got tight and I made a mistake and caught for speeding."

Just inside 100 laps to go, he was lapped by leader and eventual winner Kasey Kahne. Earnhardt returned to the lead lap by virtue of the free pass rule on lap 345 and wound up with a 14th-place finish.

"Between the tightness and the poor track position, we really struggled for a while. I had a tough time getting the car to turn, and when I did, we were behind so many cars that it was hard to gain any ground.

"We lost a lap but made it up pretty quickly when we were the 'lucky dog.' Pete and the team made the car drive better. I think we might have had a 10th-place car, but I'll take the 14th."

The stretch that began with such high hopes then ended on a sour note in the All-Star Challenge.

Earnhardt started 20th and saw his chances of a victory evaporate when he became involved in a multi-car crash on lap 35 that began when Joe Nemechek and Kevin Harvick came together coming out of turn four.

Earnhardt continued to the end in his battered car and finished 10th among the 10 cars that were running at the finish.

"We tried to tape up the front end and fix it," Earnhardt said. "But it must have been something in the suspension when we slid through the grass and kept banging around."

But, his all-star weekend gave no hint of the radical change the team would make before it retuned for the Coca-Cola 600 the next week.

Crew Switch Announcement from January

When the 2004 NASCAR NEXTEL Cup season ended, all seemed rosy for Dale Earnhardt Jr. and his No.8 Budweiser Chevrolet team.

He ended the season with a personal-best six wins. He qualified for the Chase for the NASCAR NEXTEL Cup, stayed in serious contention all the way through the 10-race playoff and wound up finishing fifth in points.

But, all was not as sunny as it seemed.

Earnhardt put together the best season of his career despite being terribly inconsistent.

Of the six wins, two came in the continuation of his prowess in restrictor-plate races since 2001, another was a second straight win at Phoenix and another came at Bristol, where he had run strongly in the past.

On the other side of the ledger, he continued to run poorly at most of the moderately banked 1.5-mile and 2 mile tracks plus the 2.5-mile triangle at Pocono. The exception to the rule came at Atlanta, where he won in the spring and was in contention to win before crashing in the fall.

When things didn't go well, he continued to have heated arguments was his cousin and car chief Tony Eury Jr. as they at times blended no better together that oil and water. Despite having one of the best seasons of any team, the decision was made to shake things up to improve the performance of Earnhardt and teammate Michael Waltrip, who finished 2004 winless.

In the biggest bombshell of the offseason, the two drivers swapped crews and cars in the hopes of making enough changes that would give Earnhardt the extra ingredients to win the championship and put Waltrip back in victory lane.

With the move, Earnhardt found himself with a crew chief other than his uncle Tony Eury Sr. for the first time since Earnhardt started racing on the NASCAR Busch Series in 1998.

Eury Sr. took a management position while helping call the shots on Waltrip's team while Eury Jr. was given the title of Waltrip's crew chief. Pete Rondeau, a New Englander with a more even temperament than Eury Jr., became Earnhardt's crew chief.

When the team rolled into Daytona in January for off-season testing, Earnhardt said his relationship with Eury Jr. wasn't as bad as he sometime portrayed it to be, but that the change was made was to help both to become more balanced in handling problems

"We were kind of holding each other back," Earnhardt said. "He had a lot of talent that wouldn't come to the surface because of our mentality toward each other. I have a lot of maturing to do as far as working with someone I'm forced to respect. I could say anything to Tony Jr. because I knew the next day we would still be cousins."

Earnhardt said the decision to switch wasn't the result of any comments that he made.

"It wasn't a situation that was so bad that I said, 'I have to get out of here.' I wasn't necessarily the guy who spoke first about it. I came into the shop and we looked at few scenarios. I walked in one day and it was all figured out. I said 'OK, I'm fine with this.'"

Rondeau said he didn't see any changes coming.

"They called me to (DEI general manager) Richie Gilmore's office," Rondeau recalled. "Earnhardt was sitting there. They asked me if I wanted the job. I said 'Yes'".

Earnhardt said he agreed to the change because he and Eury Jr. needed to become more polished in working with people.

"I put myself in this position so I could be a better person and a little more professional," he said. "I was a good race driver, but I wasn't a professional talking on the radio to the crew.

"For Tony, it will open a lot of doors in becoming a people person. He's going to have to understand to motivate people. For him, it is now or never. He won't have the opportunity when he is older because he won't change."

Rondeau thought the lack of a family tie with Earnhardt would help.

"It might be easier communicating and stepping on each other's toes because we are not family.

"I expect him to be straight-forward with me, and I am going to be straight-forward with him. I worked hard at doing that with the guys. I told them to be straight-forward with him and let him know everything we wants to know. Our relationship is going to be better if we are straight up with each other.

During the practice session at Daytona,

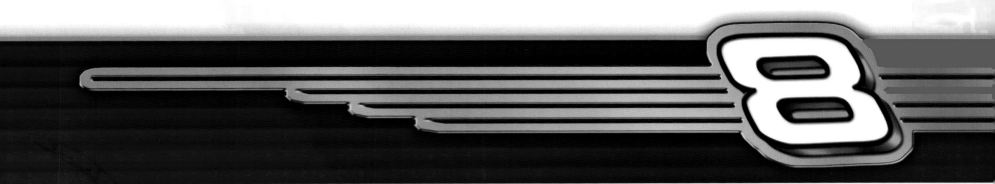

Earnhardt said he missed some things that he liked about working with his cousin.

"But, working with Pete is what I need to do. Working in that environment with my new crew is what I need to turn the corner. I don't think anything I was doing in the past kept me from winning the championship, but this is what I need to get there. Hopefully, I'm right."

He talked positively about getting off on the right foot with Rondeau, who raced 18 years in Late Models and Modified in Northeast. He served on Waltrip's team for three seasons and became crew chief when Slugger Labbe left near the end of 2004.

"One thing I like about Pete is he gives me a lot of respect," Earnhardt said. "When we talk, we listen. He has a similar demeanor as I do around the shop and away from the track. . . The work I've seen the guys do so far under Pete is really satisfying to me. They keep their heads down and keep working on things that we need to improve."

But, he conceded that the change would be no piece of cake and was ready for the negative reaction if it didn't work out.

"People are going to talk one way or another," Earnhardt said. "If Tony Jr. and I had stayed together, they would have said something. When we would get inconsistent, they would talk and try to figure out who was at fault. It's tough when you walk around in that red uniform. It was hard on Tony Jr. and Tony Sr. and that crew because they wanted to stay in their own little world.

"There is a lot of pressure and I can see this going either way. Eventually we'll do what it takes to get it right. It we start out stumbling, we'll have to do what it takes to get it right. I'm prepared for that.

"All you can do is go to the track and try your hardest. I'm doing all they can do and they are doing all they can do. When you struggle, it's not like you can look up the answer in a book."

Rondeau said he was ready for the criticism if the team did not perform up to expectations early in the season.

"I'm plenty prepared for that," Rondeau said. "If we hit it off the bat, we do. It we don't, it wouldn't be a big thing for me."

He did note that Rondeau was more of the quiet type.

"I think that Pete's got a lot on the ball. He doesn't talk a lot and it's hard to tell how much depth he has. But, he was really paying attention last year. He's got more going on his head than he shows."

Rondeau said he hoped that his more easy-going demeanor would be an advantage in keeping Earnhardt from losing his patience.

"There are times when he is going to get wound up," Rondeau said. "As a rule, I don't. It takes me a bit to get wound up. If he gets wound up, it's my job to see that he relaxes."

Rondeau did note that he had one pet peeve, people making mistakes that caused the team to do something twice.

"Even then, I don't yell and scream," he said.
The car swap meant that all Earnhardt's cars went to Waltrip's team and were change to No. 15, and all of Waltrip's cars went to Earnhardt and were changed to No. 8. Earnhardt said that his two-time winning car from Phoenix was the only one that he wanted to keep.

"I really can't tell one car from another," Earnhardt said. "They've all got tags and numbers, but I really can't tell you the difference. The Phoenix car would be nice to have back, but we can build some just like that over and over."

Earnhardt thought that the change gave him more influence at DEI.

"There are a lot of things that will change with all the moving around. I think I will be more respected within the company. I think things that I say about the car and what I ask for will carry a little more weight. Pete knows I'm the link between him and the steering wheel. Within in the company, I get a little different reaction."

Rondeau, however, said he would not make every chassis change suggested by Earnhardt during races.

"That's where our learning process is going to be as far as how he is relating to the chassis. I'm not going to say if he calls for a chassis change that I'm going to say no. But, I'm not going to do it just because he wants to do it."

Even with working out the bugs with a new crew chief, Earnhardt's approach to the season did not change.

"Just to win races is fun," Earnhardt said. "I want to contend for wins and be in the chase. I want to be a competitor and be consistently up front."

Coca Cola 600 to Sonoma

The results were not immediate.

With the removal of Pete Rondeau as crew chief, hopes ran high coming into the Coca-Cola 600 that Earnhardt would continue his move toward qualifying for the "Chase for the Championship."

Instead, he began a five a race-stretch that started and ended with two of his low points of the season, sending him from 11th in points down to 18th and far away from being within 400 points of the leader.

The positive attitude generated from the crew chief shake-up were offset two days later by an incident during the 600 that was one of the most controversial for Dale Earnhardt Inc. and ruined a strong run at Lowe's Motor Speedway.

Earnhardt began the event a little off the mark, getting lapped by lap 79 of the 400-lap event. He got back in the lead lap by virtue of the free pass rule at lap 145 and his crew had improved the Budweiser Chevrolet to the point that it was in seventh place when things fell apart.

Heading down the frontstretch of the 1.5-mile track, Earnhardt ran into the rear of teammate Michael Waltrip as they battled for sixth place. Both crashed, with Waltrip's NAPA Chevrolet damaged so badly that track workers brought it back to the garage area on a flatbed wrecker. After a lengthy time in the garage for repairs, Earnhardt returned and limped to a 33rd-place finish, his second worst of the season to that point. The crash, which helped contribute to a NASCAR NEXTEL Cup race record 22 caution periods, also took out Terry Labonte and Matt Kenseth.

"I got a real good run off the corner and tried to go to the outside of him," Earnhardt said. "I was little bit to the outside of him and the next thing I know, he's spinning. I didn't know I was close as I was to hitting him I hate it for Tony Jr. and all those guys. I just made a mistake."

Earnhardt received very little sympathy from Tony Eury Sr. as crewmen maneuver Waltrip's car into its hauler.

"It seems that Earnhardt gets into Michael every time he gets around him," Eury Sr. "I don't know why that is, but we are going to find out in the morning at the shop."

Earnhardt said he understood Tony Sr.'s point of view but insisted he had no feud brewing with Waltrip.

"There's no problem between me and Michael," Earnhardt said. "He's definitely not the person I wanted to run into. I know some of the guys on Michael's team are probably upset. But, if you are not in the race car, then you don't know what is going on out on the track."

Earnhardt contended that Waltrip was in the wrong place at the wrong time.

"He's just happened to be the guy I was out there racing," Earnhardt said. "It could have been anybody. He was the last person I wanted to run into, but we were all going for the same piece of real estate."

At the time of the wreck, Earnhardt was running his fastest laps of the night. He was pleased with the improvements that interim crew chief Steve Hmiel made to the car.

"The communication between us was awesome," Earnhardt said. "We kept getting the car better and better. We hadn't run laps below 30 seconds all night and right before the wreck we were running 29.6's. We were a half-second faster than he had been all night. I felt like we let one slip away. We could have had a top five or even a victory tonight."

Things didn't get much better when he finished 22nd and three laps down to winner Greg Biffle the next week at Dover. Earnhardt said his car bounced so violently on the mile rack's rough concrete surface that he was sore after the race.

"I felt like I was in a paint-can shaker with a cinder block tied to my back. The car bounced and bounced through the corners, and no matter what we did, the bounce didn't go away."

Earnhardt found nothing to put in a positive light after failing to be competitive on a track where he tasted the sweet fruits of victory in 2001.

"It wasn't much fun out there," he said. "We never could make the car work through the corners. It was the worst on the last two runs and I thought for sure I was going to be a crashing."

"We've got to get better and we know it."

Then came a 33rd at Pocono when he was once again the victim of tire trouble, blowing two right fronts, part of a total of 23 flats as some drivers had as many as five come apart in the race won by Carl Edwards.

Earnhardt suffered his first flat on lap 58 and the other tire blew 10 laps later. The second tire shredded to the point that it left debris on the track. As Earnhardt made his way to the pits, his exposed left-front wheel began

scraping the ground and eventually locked up. Sparks from the dragging wheel ignited and fire raged within the wheel well as Earnhardt neared his stall. Earnhardt's crew needed track workers to extinguish the fire before making repairs.

"It's hard to find anything positive about a day like this one," Earnhardt said. "It has been a struggle all season and Sunday was another frustrating day. We had those flats and we fixed the car as best we could and made laps. The only thing you can do is put it behind you."

He hung on to finish 17th and in the lead lap at Michigan. He ran as high as 15th and as low as 24th.

"Everybody earned their pay today," Earnhardt said after the race. "We had a car that was really fast during several segments of the race and we were able to run with the leaders when we restarted as the first lapped car.

"If we keep bringing stuff like this to the track, we'll get it sooner or later. I think we learned some things about the chassis. We were absolutely as fast as anybody in the corners, but they'd go past us on the straights, I wouldn't be surprised if we found something in the intake. It just wasn't pulling I was straight-out getting' kicked on the straights.

He was lapped at lap 140 but got back on the lap with the leader at lap 168.

"We would have been the lucky dog earlier and that would have helped us pass a lot more guys. But, the crew gave me a great pit stop and we were able to be the first car to restart one lap down. Then we ran away until the next yellow flag came out."

The progress at Michigan was wiped out the next Sunday at Infineon Raceway when Earnhardt's transmission came apart just after the start.

Slowing when he was left without any gears, Earnhardt got in the way of Mike Bliss and then spun into the wall on the frontstretch as he started the third lap. After repairs, he completed the race and finished 42nd.

"I just couldn't get of the way," Earnhardt said. "My car wasn't in gear when I got hit. That transmission must have been made of aluminum. It tore all to heck.

Earnhardt was not pleased with the turn of events.

"I'm just frustrated that we put ourselves in this position. We are in control of his. We need to not make these mistakes. The transmission was a new trick one and it didn't; work. Last year's transmission was pretty good."

Pepsi 400 to Brickyard 400

Dale Earnhardt Jr. found the deck stacked against him.

Nothing heading into the USG Sheetrock 400 indicated that Budweiser Chevrolet would pull into victory lane at Chicagoland Speedway.

Very few times during the season had Earnhardt been in contention outside of the restrictor plate races, and some of the teams worst struggles had come on the 1.5-mile race tracks like Chicagoland.

Most of the way through the 400-mile contest there was little to suggest the No.8 would pull into victory lane.

No one could keep pace with Matt Kenseth, one of Earnhardt's closest friends on the circuit.

After taking the lead on lap 65, Kenseth was out of the lead only during pit stops until a caution with a little over 20 laps to go in the 267-lap race. That's when Earnhardt and crew chief Steve Hmiel made a gamble that came up all aces.

They chose to take two tires and were second on the ensuing restart behind Scott Wimmer, who did not pit. Kenseth restarted in eighth.

Once he disposed of Wimmer, Earnhardt took advantage of running in clear air to streak to the 16th victory of his career and first since Talladega last October, helped by a caution with 10 laps to go that delayed Kenseth's charge out of the pack. As it was, Kenseth fell only .4 of a second short at the finish.

"I've never won a race like that," Earnhardt said. "I've lost some races like that. I was amazed that it paid off."

Earnhardt said he called for the two-tire stop when he and Hmiel discussed strategy.

"Matt had the best car hands down," Earnhardt said. "I was sitting there riding along, hoping to finish the race without any cautions because I thought we were fortunate to be in the top five and a top five finish would be great for our team. The caution came out and I asked Steve what he wanted to do. I said I know a lot of guys are going to take two tires toward the front. If you put me in front with two tires, maybe I can hold them off - maybe it would take a while for those guys with four tires to get through the field and we'll have a chance to get away from them a little bit. Steve agreed and made the call to do it. And we took off there. By the time Matt was clear in second place, I was far enough ahead. But I still thought he would catch me and we would get beat on the last lap or with two (laps) to go."

Earnhardt credited improvements to his car implemented by Hmiel as the reason he was in contention at the end.

"When Steve came on, he saw a lot of things. And it took three or four weeks for him to change what he saw," Earnhardt said. "(Former car chief) Tony Eury Jr. and Steve have a real good working relationship. Tony Jr. and that team deserve the credit. They've been innovative and found a lot of things while we were steadily getting further behind in our predicament the first three months of the season. They were gaining and learning.

"Steve asked Tony Jr. some questions and applied some ideas. The first time I felt like we were going to the race track with some footing was at Michigan. The car was strong. We had a fast car. We were starting to get some grip and see some improvement and that's exactly what happened. So I'm not real surprised. Obviously we can all stand here and say this is a fifth place car today. We would have been happy with that. We gained all day. We just made the calls that a guy with this much experience can make. We put ourselves in position to win. Today it paid off."

With the win, Earnhardt moved into 13th in points and within 112 points of 10th-place Kurt Busch with eight races left to quality for the NASCAR NEXTEL Cup.

Earnhardt said he adjusted his attitude about the Chase a week earlier as he prepared for the Pepsi 400 at Daytona.

"I changed my attitude a little bit and quit worrying about it," he said. "I started thinking more about each lap and each position and being a little more basic about it. It helps. It keeps you motivated. Races like this helps."

His run at Daytona mirrored his day in the Daytona 500 five months earlier, coming away with a third-place finish after taking his lumps in qualifying.

Earnhardt started 39th and went to the back of the field again after bouncing off Matt Kenseth as they scraped past a multi-car wreck in turn four on lap 35 of the 160-lapper that was delayed almost two hours by rain.

"It didn't do anything suspension wise or knock the toe in or anything," Earnhardt said. "It was a hard hit. Everybody started wrecking and I went low. The guys on the inside stayed straight and Matt and I were both going low. Jamie (McMurray) was already under the commitment line going on pit road and Matt and me were both coming toward down to him and I was just meeting a sandwich. I had to hit one of them, so I hit Matt."

The Budweiser Chevrolet finally cracked the top 10 after 85 laps and following a lap 115 restart, Earnhardt surged from ninth to second in just 16 laps. He was fifth on a restart with nine laps to go, and with help of longtime rival Rusty Wallace passed Jamie McMurray and Kasey Kahne on the final lap.

"We fought real hard all night and got better track position as the night went on," Earnhardt said. "And, I got some unexpected help from one of my most fierce competitors right there at the end. I was telling everybody before that restart, that I don't think Rusty's ever bump drafted me in my career. He's always trying to pass me because we were such competitors,

corporately. He decided to tell me, from spotter to spotter, that he would help me. So, that was awesome at the end."

Earnhardt cautioned against becoming overly optimistic that the third-place would provide any momentum to make the Chase.

"I understand this is Daytona and there aren't any more Daytonas and Talladegas before the Chase. We have to work really hard to gain ground on these other tracks we haven't had success yet this year."

After the win at Chicago, the outlook for making the Chase looked sunnier when the team arrived at New Hampshire Speedway's flat mile track.

He fought an ill-handling car in the early stages of the 300-lap event, dropping as far back as 35th. With some pit stop strategy that included fuel only on one stop and a two-tire stop on another, Earnhardt climbed toward the front of the field.

He was in 12th by lap 215 and down the stretch passed Jimmie Johnson and the ailing car of Jeff Gordon to finish ninth, his third straight top-10.

"We were just a little bit off today," Earnhardt said. "I would have liked a little bit better car. We tried and tried and adjusted on it a lot. But we couldn't get that extra step we needed to be able to get a top five. But we held our own today and had to drive real hard every lap and hopefully that's enough."

He told the crew near the midway point that a new seat installed for this race was uncomfortable and he got out of the Budweiser Chevrolet limping a bit.

"It's a brand new car with a brand new seat and all that," Earnhardt said. "We've just got to work the bugs out of it. You get sore when you get a new seat and you can't really figure out where it hurts until you get out and race it."

With the finish Earnhardt remained in 13th place in the points, but moved within 59 points of tenth with seven races left to qualify for the chase.

"Obviously my situation looks a heck of a lot better than it did six weeks ago. We were on our way out at a fast pace, and now we seem

to be climbing back. Hopefully we have what it takes. It's going to take some hard work."

The scramble to make the Chase was dealt a blow the next week at Pocono when Earnhardt finished 32nd, two laps down to Kurt Busch at the end of a 500-mile race. Earnhardt lost both laps in the pits, one of them on a penalty for speeding exiting the pits in an attempt to get out ahead of the pace car. Earnhardt was clocked at 143 miles an hour, far faster than the pit road speed limit of 55 miles an hour.

"I'm sorry because that was stupid to go that fast down through there with all those guys on pit road," Earnhardt radioed his crew. "Tell (NASCAR president) Mike Helton and all those officials that I'm sorry."

Starting 38th, he fell a lap down when the caution came out just as he completed a green flag stop. Then came the speeding violation, trying to stay one-lap down while the team changed the right-front spring under caution.

The spring change was part of some major adjustments that enabled the No.8 Chevrolet to go from far off the pace at the start to one of the fastest cars at the end of the 500-miler.

The finish dropped Earnhardt to 14th in points and 110 out of tenth.

"It was kind of a rough start, but once we got the car figured out, it was easy," Earnhardt said. "We learned some stuff today. At the beginning of the weekend, we were really bad. But at the end of the race, we were really fast. We got some stuff figured out. I can't wait for Indy."

Earnhardt's upbeat outlook for the Allstate 400 at the Brickyard and chances for making the Chase were quickly dashed at the historic Indianapolis Motor Speedway.

He started 27th and was unable to advance before suffering a blow that ended his day on lap 62 of the 160-lap event.

As cars stacked up on a restart, Mike Skinner ran into the back of the No.8 Chevrolet into the inside wall. Earnhardt bounced back into traffic, collecting his DEI teammate Martin Truex Jr. and Scott Wimmer.

After looking at the damage, the decision was made that the Budweiser Chevy would not return, dooming Earnhardt to a 43rd place finish in the 43-car field.

"Everybody took off and then everybody stopped, and when I stopped I got ran into,' Earnhardt said. "It's hard to see what the leaders are doing when you are in the back. But, they called the green flag and I was waiting for Bill (Elliott) to go and when Bill took off, I took off and we stopped again. I don't think Skinner knew what was going on. And I got turned into the wall."

The finish dropped Earnhardt to 16th in standings, but more importantly, left him 191 out of 10th with five races left before the chase.

"I ain't a fortune teller but things aren't looking good," He said. "We are way behind and there aren't many races left."

Watkins Glen to Richmond

Smoke and steam billowed from the rear of the Budweiser Chevrolet as it fell off the pace on California Speedway's backstretch.

A stream of oil and water trailed from the red No. 8 as it coasted into the garage area, indicating its run in the 500-mile race had come to an end.

When he climbed out of the driver's window, Earnhardt knew that he was mathematically eliminated from qualifying for the Chase for the NASCAR NEXTEL Cup even though the identity of all ten drivers who would qualify for the playoff would not be decided until the next week's race at Richmond.

In view of the team's disappointing performances throughout the season, Earnhardt then made assured his supporters of one thing.

"I promise my fans I'll be back in Victory Lane," Earnhardt said.

Less than two weeks later, steps were put into motion to accomplish that goal when Tony Eury Jr. was returned to the Budweiser team and made Earnhardt's crew chief, undoing the off-season change in which Tony Jr. was shifted to Michael Waltrip's team in a total swap of crews.

Earnhardt's performance suffered because of the crew shift and when he failed to make the Chase, the move was made to put Eury in charge of Earnhardt's cars in an effort to get ready for 2006. The reunion had been expected for weeks.

"We could have made this change earlier, but Michael and Tony Jr. were enjoying themselves so it wouldn't have been fair to them," Earnhardt said. "They deserved it. But, when it got to the point that neither of us got to the Chase, it was time to work toward next year."

Earnhardt said that Eury has given his team advice at the shop and at the track throughout the season.

"It's not like I hadn't seen him for eight months," Dale said. "The biggest thing in our relationship now is we have more respect for each other."

When he dropped out of the California race, Earnhardt said he realistically felt for several weeks that he would not qualify for the Chase.

"We quit worrying about points a long time ago," Earnhardt said.

His chances of making the Chase began looking slim when he crashed at Indianapolis. But a 10th at Watkins Glen, an 18th at Michigan and a ninth at Bristol kept the possibility of a chase berth alive.

At Watkins Glen, Earnhardt needed the whole race to bounce back for pitting just before an early caution fell during a sequence of green flag stops, leaving him near the rear of the field? He passed six cars in the closing laps to come away with the top-ten finish.

"It's better than what I thought we would get, and the team is happy with it," Earnhardt said. "I'm real upset that I got into Dale Jarrett and spun him out near the end, That's bothering me because we are real good friends."

In the 400-mile race at Michigan, he was one of the losers in a late fuel mileage battle after running from between seventh and 12th for most of the last 220 miles. He actually led a lap in the late sequence of stops before pitting with eight laps to go.

"I hate fuel mileage races where the fastest car doesn't win," Earnhardt said. "A had a heck of a good time racing three-wide for most of the race, but it gives you a sick feeling that once you make that last stop, you hope that everyone else has to stop."

Earnhardt was pleased with his car for most of the race, saying that it was almost perfect at a couple of points.

"It got better and better all afternoon and then we struggled on the last set of tires (taken with 56 laps to go)," he said. "It got really, really bad at the end. It was like we had something to happen with a spring or a shock."

He roared the next week into Bristol, one of his favorite tracks, with hopes of repeating as winner of the Sharpie 500.

Earnhardt had to start at the rear of the field because the fuel pressure gauge was replaced after qualifying, more than the work allowed under impound rules.

He benefited from the lucky dog rule three times in the first 150 laps to stay on the lead lap, but finally gained enough track position to the point that getting lapped was no longer a worry. He also drove through a couple of wrecks that caused no significant damage to the Budweiser Chevrolet.

A quick pit stop with 80 laps to go boosted Earnhardt into the top 10 for the first time. From there, he endured pressure from several cars to finish ninth. He also retained a shot at making the chase by drawing within 117 points of tenth place.

"I know people are wondering how we got a top-10 finish, but the Budweiser Chevy was fast tonight and we passed a lot of people.

He also thought that deciding not to pit with 28 laps to go to hold onto ninth was a key.

"I knew it would be hard to hold off the guys who changed tires," Earnhardt said. "I was kind of mad at myself for not stopping. But track position is real important here because it is so hard to pass."

Then came the bad night at California when another good one was needed. Earnhardt said his engine started going sour long before it came apart.

"It ran terrible most of the night," Earnhardt said. "I was getting killed on the straights. The way it was running rough, I knew about 80 laps before it blew up that we weren't going to make the Chase. I'm disappointed with the way we ran, but it's been like that the most of the year."

That left winning as his primary objective beginning the next week at Richmond as most attention was centered on those trying to make the chase. He wound up finishing 20th after being one of the parts of the sandwich in a crash with 45 laps to go.

Even though it appeared that he escaped with little damage, the Budweiser Chevy was a handful to drive the rest of the night on the way to finishing 20th.

"It was like it was possessed," Earnhardt said. "It was like it had a mind of its own. I'm not pleased with the finish, but I like how hard the team worked."

Then came the announcement three days later that Tony Jr. was his crew chief again, giving Earnhardt much to look forward to for 2006.

Daytona International Speedway

DAYTONA 500
FEBRUARY 20, 2005

Dale Earnhardt Jr. shoots ahead of Kasey Kahne (9) and Scott Riggs (10) in his run toward the front. After a pit stop a little over 30 laps from the end, Earnhardt charged from 17th to 5th place between a restart on Lap 173 and the time the caution flag waved on Lap 184. Following another yellow that began on Lap 189, Earnhardt and Tony Stewart swapped the lead from Laps 195-197 before Jeff Gordon went in front to stay on Lap 198 by blowing past on the backstretch. Earnhardt lost second place to Kurt Busch in a green-white-checkered finish and wound up third.

[Above] The Budweiser Chevrolet crew gives Earnhardt four fresh tires and a tank of fuel during a critical pit stop in the waning laps. After battling an ill-handling car, Earnhardt challenged his crew to get it fixed on the last two stops. "I told them they had to get the thing freed up so it would turn," Earnhardt said. "They did exactly what I told them to do. I had one of the best cars out there at the end of the race."

[Right] Earnhardt (left) talks with cousin and former car chief Tony Eury Jr. in the Daytona garage area. After a 2005 campaign which ended with the pair barely on speaking terms, they were separated when Earnhardt and teammate Michael Waltrip swapped crew members. Despite the split, Earnhardt continued to seek advice from Eury Jr. By the end of the season, they were back together with Eury Jr. as Earnhardt's crew chief.

Earnhardt sweeps to the inside of Kasey Kahne (9) and Joe Nemechek (01) in three-abreast racing. This is typical of the action in restrictor-plate events at Daytona and Talladega where the entire field runs virtually the same speed in the draft. Earnhardt stayed in the middle of the pack most of the day, saying at one point that the car drove like it had a hole in the nose and that he was lucky to keep up with the draft. After a late pit stop, he rallied and came away with a third-pace finish in the world's most famous stock-car race.

California Speedway

AUTO CLUB 500
FEBRUARY 27, 2005

Dale Earnhardt Jr. zips along the long frontstretch at California Speedway. Although the Budweiser Chevrolet crew had struggled with handling troubles at the two-mile track in recent races, Earnhardt said his Chevrolet handled well, even after damage caused by the second of two flat tires that occurred 22 laps apart. The team went without tire trouble the rest of the day. "That was weird," Earnhardt said. "We didn't change air pressure or anything and the flats just stopped."

Earnhardt blasts through a turn at Caifornia Speedway during the Auto Club 500. The 500-mile race was seen as the first big test for the Budweiser Chevrolet crew because of medicore performance on intermediate tracks such as the two-mile oval located in the Los Angeles suburb of Fontana. Earnhardt was fast at the start, moving from 40th starting posiiton into the top 25 before the day was derailed by a pair of flat left-front tires. The first came on lap 36. The second one came apart 22 laps later and shredded the left front fender. He fell one lap behind during the pit stop to replace the first flat and lost several more laps during the repair of damage caused by the second flat. When it was over, Earnhardt settled for a 32nd-place finish, 13 laps behind winner Greg Biffle.

Wearing sunglasses, Earnhardt sports the perefect look for southern California as he awaits his turn in qualifying. Earnhardt qualified 40th and wound up apologizing to the crew for making a mistake that kept him from bagging a top-10 starting position.

Las Vegas Motor Speedway

UAW-DALMIER CHRYSLER 400

MARCH 13, 2005

Dale Earnhardt Jr. leads Brian Vickers (black car,right), Rusty Wallace (white hood), Bobby Labonte (green car) and Ricky Rudd (red car) early in the Uaw-Daimler Chrysler 400. Vickers followed Earnhardt for three laps before Earnhardt let the second-year driver complete a pass. Shortly after that going into turn one on lap 12, Earnhardt clipped the rear of Vickers' car going into turn one. Earnhardt tried to squeeze between Vickers's spinning car and the outside wall without success and was knocked into the barrier. When the crashing was over, Labonte and Ricky Rudd were also collected. Labonte, Earnhardt and Vickers were sidelined, finishing 41st- 43rd respectively. Rudd returned after 80 laps behind the wall. Earnhardt apologized to Vickers for helping cause the wreck.

Smokes streams from the Budweiser Chevrolet in the wake of Earnhardt's colliding with Brian Vickers heading into turn one at Las Vegas Motor Speedway. With his damaged car sliding on a track that was slick outside of the groove, Earnhardt could not avoid a second collision with Vickers and a meeting with the outside wall. The crashes battered the front and rear of the Bud Chevrolet, inflicting damage that the DEI crew could not repair at the track.

Earnhardt runs down Las Vegas Speedway's banking as he sprints away from a badly mangled Budweiser Chevrolet while traffic passes to the outside. The damage too severe to be fixed, relegating Earnhardt to a 42nd place in another disappointing day on the 1.5-mile track. The poor finish left sent him plummeting from 14th to a season-low 27th in the points, leaving a sizable mountain to overcome in a quest for a berth in the Chase for the NASCAR NEXTEL Cup.

Atlanta Motor Speedway

GOLDEN CORRAL 500
MARCH 20, 2005

Dale Earnhardt Jr. pulls into his pit stall as his crew springs into action beginning with a four-tire change. Tape on the pavement and a sign attached to a pole tell Junior where to stop the Budweiser Chevrolet at the point that is best for his crew and to get out of the pits with the least trouble.

Budweiser
Bud
Snap-on
MENARDS
CHAMPION
NAPA
8
DaleEarnhardtInc.com
Budweiser
Budweiser.com
NAPA
Miller Welders
RITZ CRACKERS
Snap-on
EAGLE
GOODYEAR
8

Earnhardt ís crew leaps into action during the Golden Corral 500. The pit work was outstanding throughout the race, but Earnhardt received two drive-though penalties for speeding on pit road. The extra time in the pits dropped him two laps down, a deficit that he could not erase while fitting a car that was very loose in the turns. The combination of the penalties and the car left Junior with a disappointing 24th place finish in an event he won in 2005. He took full responsibility for costing the team a better finish.

Bristol Motor Speedway

FOOD CITY 500

APRIL 3, 2005

Dale Earnhardt Jr. hugs the inside line as he rounds one of Bristol's steeply banked turns. Because speeds are so fast, cars are virtually impossible to pass if they stick in the inside groove. Helped by some drivers having tire trouble down the stretch, Earnhardt managed to gain several spots as he moved from 19th to inside the top-10 in the first 78 laps and picked up three positiions in the last 12 laps.

Earnhardt leads a line of cars on one of Bristol straight-aways. Because speeds are so fast, giving drivers little time to react, being at the front is one of the safest places to be at Bristol. Those in the pack have little time to take action avoiding a spinning car, many times leading to a simple one-car spin turning into a multi-car pileup. The Food City 500 was plagued by wrecks that led to a total of 14 cautions. The worst crash was a 10-car pile-up that brought out the red flag. While the race was stopped, a crew member checked one of Earnhardt's tires to make sure they were not flat-spotted when he slammed on the brakes to avoid Matt Kenseth's spinning car.

Earnhardt came into the Food City 500 seeking his second straight Bristol Motor Speedway victory. Despite failing to repeat, Earnhardt was thrilled to post a fourth-place finish, his second top five of the year, on a day when wrecks and tire troubles took out a number of contenders.

Martinsville Speedway

ADVANCE AUTO PARTS 500

APRIL 10, 2005

Very few cars escape Martinsville Speedway's tight short-track turns without some sheet metal damage, and the No.8 Budweiser Chevrolet was no exception in the Advance Auto Parts 500. Dale Earnhardt Jr. completed less than a lap before receiving front fender damage in a multi-car chain reaction in Turns three and four that dropped him to 40th place. He battled an early fender rub for about 50 laps and became involved in a number of incidents, eventually spinning coming off Turn two on Lap 288. With almost 50 laps to go, a rub from Travis Kvapil knocked Junior's fender against his right-rear tire, causing enough damage that Junior was unable to mount a charge down the stretch. Through it all, he stayed on the lead lap and managed a 13th-place finish.

Earnhardt's helmet sits atop the Budweiser Chevrolet, waiting for him to don it at a practice session. As much protection as possible was needed in the Advance Auto Parts 500, which was plauged by 16 caution periods and had a crash on the very first lap.

[Right] It's a meeting of the Dales. Earnhardt talks with Dale Jarrett before practice. Jarrett is a long time friend of the Earnhardt family and traditionally allows Earnhardt to hitch a ride on his helicopter to the Martinsville track. Ironically, Earnhardt passed Jarrett following a restart with three laps to go to win a battle for 13th-place in the Advance Auto Parts 500.

Texas Motor Speedway

SAMSUNG/RADIO SHACK 500

APRIL 17, 2005

Dale Earnhardt Jr. has a concerned look on his face as he tries to figure out chassis changes that will make the No.8 Budweiser Chevrolet handle better Texas offered an opportunity for a breakthrough as it is one of Earnhadts's favorite and was the scene of his first NASCAR NEXTEL Cup Series victory in 2000. He responded with his best intermediate track run of the season, working his way into the top five before pitting for the last time on Lap 298 of the 334-lapper. Junior's handling wasn't quite the same down the stretch as he dropped to a ninth-place finish.

The No.8 Budwesier crew goes to work as they hustle through a four-tire pit stop. Despite troubles on the track, Earnhardt praised his crew's fast stops that enabled him to stay on the lead lap and eventually crack the top five before settling for a ninth-place finish, his third top-10 effort of the year.

Crewemembers push the No.8 Budweiser Chevrolet into the qualifying line for the Samsung/Radio Shack 500. Earnhardt qualified 11th, one of his best efforts of the year and finished ninth.

Phoenix International Speedway

SUBWAY FRESH 500

APRIL 23, 2005

Dale Earnhardt Jr. leads Joe Nemechek, Jimmie Johnson and Ryan Newman through a Phoenix turn. In the early laps, Earnhardt found it difficult getting through the turns when he tried to pick up his pace. After adjusting his driving style by not charging through the corners, he started passing cars, eventually settling into the top five and coming away with a fourth place finish.

[Left] Earnhardt had good reason to smile before taking the green flag at Phoenix International Raceway. He came into the Subway Fresh 500 seeking his third straight win at the one-mile almost flat track. Even though the car he drove in those victories went to Michael Waltrip in the off-season team swap, Junior showed that driver skill played a factor in those wins as he steered his new wheels to a fourth-place finish in the facility's first NASCAR NEXTEL Cup night race in the spring. It was his third top-five of the season. The event also turned out to be the best of the early season for Dale Earnhardt Inc. as Waltrip drove Junior's former car to second place finish.

[Right] Earnhardt and Matt Kenseth share a moment together before the start. Kenseth has remained one of Earnhardt's closest friends since their battle for the 2000 Raybestos Rookie of the Year honors that went to Kenseth by 42 points after Earnhardt won two of the first 16 races. Earnhardt frequently makes a point to sit with Kenseth during pre-race driver meetings.

The No.8 Budweiser pit crew hustles through a stop that helped Earnhardt maintain track position helping set up his fourth-place finish. After the race, Earnhardt lauded the crew's effort.

Talladega Superspeedway

AARON'S 499

MAY 1, 2005

Waiting for practice to begin, Dale Earnhardt Jr. stands at the opening to his garage stall and takes a look at Talladega Superpseedway. This is where he supplanted his father as king of the draft which is crucial to success at the mammoth 2.66-mile track. Coming into the Aaron's 499, Earnhardt had clicked off five wins in seven races since the track's fall race in 2001. That began a track-record string of four wins in a row that was snapped by Earnhardt's teammate Michael Waltrip in the fall of 2003. While most drivers dread racing at Talladega because of the threat of big pileups, Earnhardt enjoys it as any other track in the series.

[Above] Earnhardt and teammate Michael Waltrip race side-by-side while working the all important draft at Talladega. Junior started 36th and Waltrip 38th in a repeat of their poor qualifying effort at the Daytona 500, the year's only previous restrictor plate racing. Just as at Daytona, Earnhardt predicted their cars would draft well and he was right. Earnhardt managed to work into the lead for three laps at the half-way point. Waltrip blew past Jeff Gordon and took the lead on Lap 183 of the scheduled 188-lap race. Gordon hustled past Waltrip two laps later and won his second straight Talladega spring race. Earnhardt was invovled in a wreck on Lap 187 that sent the event into overtime. He limped to a 15th-place finish in a hastily repaired car.

[Left] Tony Eury Jr. (right) gives cousin Dale Earnhardt Jr. a shot in the ribs as they kid around during qualifying for the Aaron's 499. Friends since childhood, they remained close even though Eury, was shifted to Michael Waltrip's team in the offseason.

[Right] Earnhardt and Michael Waltrip worked the draft as Tony Stewart follows. Dale Jr. and Waltrip were not as dominant at Talladega as in previous years, when they ran in the top two poitions at will. At the end, Earnhardt wasn't a factor because of a wreck and Stewart and Waltrip were chasing leader and eventual winner Jeff Gordon. Even with Waltrip pushing Stewart on the final lap, they were unable to make a move on Gordon.

[Below] Members of the No.8 crew do their best to patch the Budweiser Chevrolet after a wreck on Lap 187. Their hard work helped secure a finish. Earnhardt blamed Jimmie Johnson for causing the wreck which also involved Martin Truex Jr., Greg Biffle, Kevin Harvick and Travis Kvapil. Truex and Johnson were unable to continue.

Darlington Raceway

DODGE CHARGER 500

MAY 7, 2005

Earnhardt passes Bobby Labonte in a battle among drivers who had endured their share of early season troubles coming into the first night race and first race on Mother's Day weekend at Darlington Raceway. Earnhardt came into the Dodge Charger 500 9th in points as his team continued to show improvement from the opening weeks of the season. The upswing continued as he overcame a 39th place qualifying effort to move into contention for a top-10 finish. Picking up a couple of spots in a green-white-checkered finish, Earnhardt came away with an eighth-place. Labonte finished 17th, going the entire distance in a welcome change of luck after falling out of five of the first nine races.

The Budweiser Chevrolet crew hustles through a four-tire stop under the lights which happen to be the first night race in the history of Darlington Raceway.

Earnhardt leans against the wall separating the pits from the racing surface as he waits for the start of the first race held on Mother's Day weekend at Darlington Raceway.

Richmond International Raceway
CHEVY AMERICAN REVOLUTION 400
MAY 14, 2005

Earnhardt climbs aboard the Budweiser Chevrolet, sitting poised in position at the edge of its garage stall to be taken out for a spin in practice at Richmond International Raceway. Earnhardt was the defending champion in the Chevy American Revolution 400 at the three-quarter mile track, one of his favorites on the circuit. He did not run as strongly as a year earlier, but got the benefit of NASCAR's free pass rule to get back in the lead lap late and rallied to post a 14th-place finish.

Earnhardt goes past Casey Mears (41) while driving toward the front half of the pack from 27th starting position. Earnhardt fought in the middle stages to stay on the lead lap while battling a car that wouldn't turn to his liking and finished 14th. Mears finished two laps behind race winner Kasey Kahne and settled for 28th place.

Earnhardt sticks to the inside groove as he blasts through one of Richmond International Raceway's turns during the Chevy American Revolution 400. Earnhardt charged from 27th to 17th in the first then the first 10 laps, then suffered a setback when he was hit with a penalty for speeding on pit road that put him at the back of the field for a Lap 134 restart. He picked up positions but could not keep from going a lap down as Kasey Kahne and Tony Stewart set a blistering pace while battling for the lead. Dale became the beneficiary of the "lucky dog" rule to return to lead on Lap 353 and with a better handling car managed to finish 14th place.

No, it's not Darth Vader. It's Earnhardt buckling his menacing-looking black helmet as he gets ready for a practice session.

Lowe's Motor Speedway

COCA-COLA 600

MAY 29, 2005

Race weekends often seem a blur while teams go through practice, qualifying and go directly from that to preparing for the race. At Lowe's Motor Speedway, teams have the luxury of working in one the nicest garage buildings on the series, with enough bays to house the cars of all of the series regulars. Things are blurry for the No.8 team here as they quickly repair Earnhardt's car after a wreck in the Coca-Cola 600.

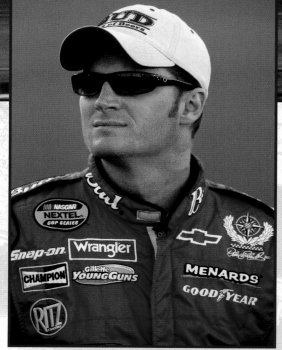

[Above] Earnhardt is trying to charge to the front as he is stuck behind a three-wide battle involving Jamie McMurray (42), Kyle Petty (45) and Jeff Burton (31).

[Right] Dale Earnhardt Jr. waits for the start of the Coca-Cola 600, which marked a fork in the road for the No.8 Dale Earnhardt Inc. team. Before qualifying for the 600-mile event, Earnhardt and DEI general manager Richie Gilmore announced DEI technical director Steve Hmiel was installed as interim crew chief. It was the first attempt to get the No.8 back on track following the swapping of cars and crews with DEI's other teams during the off season. In 11 races with Rondeau at the helm, Earnhardt had just three top-5 finishes and five top-10 finishes. He overcame a slow start to flirt with the top 10 in points. "The chemistry just wasn't there," Gilmore said. Earnhardt said he meshed well with Rondeau as a person. "We just didn't click on Sunday," Junior explained.

Earnhardt spins going into the first turn at Lowe's Motor Speedway after triggering a multi-car wreck by running into the back of his Dale Earnhardt Inc. teammate Michael Waltrip on the frontstretch. The crash sidelined Waltrip and made members of Waltrip's team livid. Among the most vocal was Tony Eury Sr., Earnhardt's former crew chief who was helping Waltrip's team as a DEI executive. Earnhardt, who returned after repairs, said he closed on Waltrip faster than expected.

Dover International Speedway
MBNA RACEPOINTS 400
JUNE 5, 2005

Dale Earnhardt Jr. and Dale Earnhardt Inc. team mate Michael Waltrip battle as they streak through one of Dover International Speedway's concrete turns. Earnhardt spent most of the day trying stay out of the way as he fought an ill-handling car that bounced so badly on both ends of the "Monster Mile" that he felt like being in a paint shaker with a cinder block tied to his back. His crew never found a solution to allow Earnhardt to run better than his 15th starting position. He fell a lap down on lap 273 and finished a disappointing 22nd in the 400-lap event. Waltrip finished 15th.

[Above] This is a worm's view of a pit stop from the rear of the Budweiser Chevrolet as fuel goes in while those changing tires sprint from the right to left side. Their quick pit work helped blunt the sting of one of Earnhardt's worst days at the Dover. His car handled badly from start to finish as his crew never came close to the combination that put Earnhardt in victory lane at the "Monster Mile" in 2001. "It's a track where we've never been consistent. Sometimes we do good, and sometimes we do bad."

[Left] The day was not one of the best for Earnhardt, but that didn't keep his crew from hustling on pit stops and trying to find a solution for the Budweiser Chevrolet's handling woes. Despite their efforts, Earnhardt said the car was at its worst following the last two pit stops. "I thought I was going to be crashing," he said. The car also bounced continually, leaving Earnhardt sore at the end.

Pocono Raceway

POCONO 500
JUNE 12, 2005

Dale Earnhardt Jr. leads a pack of cars around one of Pocono's three turns. All have different radius and degree of banking, putting passing on the straightaways at a premium. This turn has solid curbing while others had a jagged ripple strip to discourage running into the dirt on the inside of the corners. The ripple strips were blamed for some of the 22 left-front tries failures, leading track officials to replace the strips with solid curbing. Earnhardt suffered two flat left-fronts in a ten-lap span during the Pocono 500. He escaped major damage when the first one came apart. With the second one, the whole wheel area was engulfed in flames when he got to the pits. After the first was extinguished and repairs made, Junior returned to the race and continued to a 33rd-place finish, six laps down.

Earnhardt talks with third-year driver Casey Mears, the son of former IndyCar driver Roger Mears and the nephew of four-time Indianapolis 500 winner Rick Mears. Casey Mears, who came to NASCAR from the open wheel ranks, has enjoyed some of his better days at Pocono. He picked up his first NASCAR NEXTEL Cup pole there in 2004.

The Budweiser Chevrolet crew goes to work on the left front of the car after Earnhardt suffered one of his two flat left-front tires during the first 160 miles of the Pocono 500. He was more fortunate than other drivers who had as many as four tire failures.

Michigan International Speedway

BATMAN BEGINS 400

JUNE 19, 2005

Earnhardt leads a string of cars along Michigan Speedway's front stretch. Earnhardt was down on straightaway speed most of the day, leading him to believe that a problem had developed with a header.

Earnhardt leads Dale Earnhardt Inc. teammate Michael Waltrip through a Michigan Speedway turn. Waltrip had the upper hand most of the day and sprinted to a seventh-place finish. Earnhardt, handicapped by a lack of horsepower on the straightaways, finished 17th. He started 41st, moved into the top 20 in the first 40 laps, and bounced between 15th and 24th the rest of the day. He fell a lap behind at the 140-lap mark, but regained the lead lap when the yellow flag waved on lap 168.

[Above] Interim crew chief Steve Hmiel listens to Earnhardt's input during a practice for the Batman Begins 400. Hmiel, the techical driector at Dale Earnhardt Inc. who had served as Earnhardt's spotter and stepped into the crew chief's position when Pete Rondeau was reassigned in May. The team's performance gradually began improving after Hmiel took over. Hmiel got his start at Petty Enterprises and was crew chief for Kyle Petty's first win, an ARCA race at Daytona in 1979. He served on Richard Petty's crew from 1981 until going to Billy Hagan's team in 193. He was crew chief for Terry Labonte in 1985 and Sterling Marlin in 1986. He then went to Roush Racing and served as Mark Martin's crew chief from 1988-1998, guiding Martin to 27 wins. He joined Dale Earnhardt Inc. as technical director in September of 1998.

[Left] Earnhardt sits on a tool box while his DEI crew makes adjustments to the Budweiser Chevrolet during practice for the Batman Begins 400. Earnhardt finished just 17th but said the race was a step in the right direction because the crew learned things to make the car handle better.He battled poor track position most of the day, but showed that the potential of the Budweiser Chevrolet by staying with the leaders for 30 laps after restarting at the front of the line of lapped cars.

Infineon Raceway

DODGE / SAVE MART 350

JUNE 26, 2005

Dale Earnhardt Jr. crests a hill at the highest point on Infineon Raceway's 12-turn undulating road course located near the wine country of northern California and the north shore of San Francisco Bay. Drivers climb about 240 feet in elevation as they negotiate a series of curves from the start-finish line to the track's highest point. Passing is very difficult with short straightaways connecting the turns, the sharpest a hairpin that forces drivers to slow to 30 miles an hour before they roar toward the start-finish line, The track is used for a variety of racing activities for about 340 days every year.

Earnhardt spends time with his cousin and teammate Michael Waltrip's crew chief Tony Eury Jr. during a practice session. Throughout the season, the two Juniors continued to patch their differences that led to the decision to put Eury on Waltrip's team at the beginning of the year.

[Above] Crewmembers work to replace the Budweiser Chevrolet's transmission after it came apart in the first three laps of the Dodge/Save Mart 350. The transmission failure dealt a huge blow to Earnhardt's efforts to qualify for the Chase for the NASCAR NEXTEL Cup. Despite a tremendous effort by the crew to get Dale back in the race, it wasn't enough to keep him from finishing 42nd, 22 laps behind Tony Stewart and falling 543 points behind leader Greg Biffle.

[Right] Earnhardt sits in the garage area, watching intently as he watches his crew replace the transmission in the Budweiser Chevrolet. Frustrated over losing ground in the points race at a time when he needed a good finish to move closer to the top-10, Junior questioned his crew's decision at what transmission they chose. Earnhardt's troubles came on the same day that his fellow Chevrolet drivers Jeff Gordon and Jimmie Johnson encountered transmission woes.

Daytona International Speedway

PEPSI 400

JULY 2, 2005

Under the bright afternoon sun, Dale Earnhardt Jr. holds the low line in a turn while qualifying for the Pepsi 400. He qualified just 37th but had little trouble cutting through the field. His inital charge was stopped by a multi-car crash on Lap 35 that resulted in minor damage to the Budweiser Chevrolet. Earnhardt cracked the top 10 just past Lap 80 and then charged from ninth to second in 16 laps foillowing the Lap 115 restart. While the eventual winner Tony Stewart was the class of the field leading all but nine laps, Earnhardt shuffled around in the battle for second and wound up finishing third.

Earnhardt drives past Ryan Newman as they zip through one of Daytona's steeply banked turns, heading to a finish well past midnght due to a two hour rain delay. In a trend common in restrictor-plate races this season, Earnhardt qualified 37th because the Budweiser Chevrolet was slow running by itself. Running in the draft with other cars, Earnhardt once again had little trouble moving toward the front as the Budweiser crew provided another car with a good combination of handling and aerodynamics.

Earnhardt gets unexpected drafting help from his father's old foe Rusty Wallace to sweep under Jimmie Johnson as they exit turn two onto Daytona International Speedway's backstretch in the closing laps of the Pepsi 400. Wallace helped push Earnhardt past Johnson and Kasey Kahne following a late caution, helping Earnhardt to a third-place finish that tied his best for the season. Wallace traditionally refused to help Earnhardt draft at restrictor-plate races because they drive for different beer brands. But, the veteran changed his strategy in his final race at the 2.5-mile speedway.

Chicagoland Speedway

USG SHEETROCK 400

JULY 10, 2005

Chicago freight express. Dale Earnhardt Jr. is the engine at the head of a train of cars thundering around one of Chicagoland Speedway's turns. Following in order are Jason Leffler, Mark Martin, Jeremy Mayfield, Michael Waltrip and Casey Mears. Earnhardt led only 11 laps in a 400-mile race dominated most of the way by Matt Kenseth. However, it was the last 11 laps, after a gamble on a two-tire stop during a late caution period, that got Earnhardt out of the pits ahead of Kenseth and in position to win.

[Above] A jubilant Budweiser crew pushes Earnhardt's car across the infield grass toward victory lane after he celebrated his win in the USG Sheetrock 400 with burnouts. The majority of the crew had more reason to celebrate than Earnhardt. They came over to the No. 8 Budweiser Chevrolet in the off season as Earnhardt and teammate Michael Waltrip swapped crews and had not tasted victory since Waltrip won at Talladega in the fall of 2003.

[Right] Earnhardt flashes the No. 1 signal as he poses with trophy following his victory in the USC Sheetrock 400. The 16th win of Earnhardt's career extended his string to six straight seasons with at least one victory. It was also his first at Chicagoland Speedway, giving Earnhardt wins at nine tracks. The other series where Earnhardt graced victory lane include Texas, Richmond, Dover, Daytona, Talladega, Atlanta, Phoenix and Bristol.

What a relief. Earnhardt lifts his arms after climbing from his car in Chicagoland Speedway's victory lane, celebrating a surprise triumph that provided a bright spot in a season that got off to a slow start. The win was Earnhardt's first since Talladega in October of 2004 and was just his fourth top-five finish to that point in 2005. It was also not expected to come at the Chicago track, where Earnhardt's best previous finish was 10th.

New Hampshire International Speedway

NEW ENGLAND 300

JULY 17, 2005

Dale Earnhardt Jr. leads a pack of cars into a turn as he rallies from a slow start in the New England 300. Battling a car that wouldn't turn freely in the corners, Earnhardt fell to 35th in the opening laps. Using pit startegy that included a one gas-only stop and one two-tire change, Earnhardt gained enough track position to move into 12th position just past the 200-lap mark in the 300-lap race. He passed Jimmie Johnson and the ailing car of Jeff Gordon in the last 27 laps to finish ninth.

Earnhardt does his best negotiating one of New Hampshire International Speedway's flat turns. Earnhardt admitted that the Budweiser Chevrolet was quite as good as he would have liked throughout the New England 300. He said it was better at the end but his team could never get it adjusted completely. The car was new which presented another problem. Earnhardt was left sore at the end of the day because he could not get comfortable in his seat.

Earnhardt pushes the Budweiser Chevrolet in the New Hampshire International Speedway garage area. Earnhardt qualified 25th, overcame handling problems in the beginning and surged at the end to finish ninth in the New England 300. It was his third straight top-10 finish under interim crew chief Steve Hmiel.

Pocono Raceway

PENNSYLVANIA 500

JULY 24, 2005

Dale Earnhardt Jr. drives to the inside of Scott Wimmer on Pocono Raceway's Long Pond straightaway. The Budweiser Chevrolet wasn't great in the beginning, but at the end, Earnhardt was able to keep pace with the leaders while running out the final laps two laps down to leader and eventual winner Kurt Busch. "At the beginning of the weekend, we were bad, no matter what we did," Earnhardt said."But at the end, we were real fast."

Standing on pit road before the start, Earnhardt is all smiles as he waits to climb aboard the Budweiser Chevrolet. His mood was mixed after the race. He was down over losing two laps on pit road early on the way to finishing 32nd. Earnhardt lost one lap when he was caught on pit road while the caution came out as his crew changed the right front spring. He lost the another lap when he was penalized for speeding on pit road as he tried to get out ahead of the leader. But, he was upbeat over the team making the correct adjustments that transformed the Budweiser Chevrolet from a mediocre car to one of the fastest at race's end.

Earnhardt leads Brian Vickers and others around one of Pocono Raceway's three distinctive turns. This one has a vastly different look with solid white curbing installed along the edge of the track. The curbing replaced rough-edged ripple strips that were blamed for a host of flat tires in Pocono's June race. Earnhardt was of the victims of the flat tire epidemic, suffering two within a handful of laps.

Indianapolis Motor Speedway

BRICKYARD 400

AUGUST 7, 2005

Dale Earnhardt Jr. roars through one of Indianapolis Motor Speedway's four turns with three cars nipping at his bumper. Despite a good test session during his preparations for the Allstate 400 at the Brickyard, Earnhardt said his car was junk most of the time before he was sidelined by an early wreck.

Indiana crunch. With the front of the Budweiser Chevrolet dragging the ground, Earnhardt drives past the end of the pit wall and on the way to taking it directly behind the pit wall knowing his car is to smashed to continue. In a chain reaction accident on a restart, Mike Skinner sent Earnhardt sliding into the inside wall just short of the famed yard of bricks on Indianapolis Motor Speedway's front stretch. The Budweiser Chevrolet bounced off the wall and into the path of Earnhardt's DEI teammate Martin Truex Jr. and Scott Wimmer. The crash doomed Earnhardt to a 43rd-place finish and dealt a serious blow to his bid to qualify for the Chase for the NASCAR NEXTEL Cup.

Earnhardt leans against the Budweiser Chevrolet with a portion of Indianapolis Motor Speedway's massive grandstands in the background. Despite high hopes for a strong showing in front of 300,000 in one of the most prestigious races in the world, the weekend was a disappointment for Earnhardt and the Budweiser crew from the start. He qualified 27th and battled an ill-handling car from the start, routinely losing positions while his car took several laps to become suited to new tires each time. Earnhardt was beginning to the see the benefits of massive chassis changes when he was knocked into the inside wall on a restart. "We tested here and thought we had something," Earnhardt said. "But from the moment we got here, the car was junk."

Watkins Glen International

SIRIUS SATELLITE RADIO AT THE GLEN

AUGUST 14, 2005

Dale Earnhardt Jr. blasts around a turn on Watkins Glen's internationally famous road course.

Stuck in the 37th after his unfortunate timing of a pit stop before a caution period, Earnhardt methodically clawed his way toward the front. He passed six cars in the closing laps to finish 10th, his eighth top-10 finish of the season.

Earnhardt carries stern look of concentration as he focuses on matters at hand during Watkins Glen practice session. Coming off the terrible turn of luck at Indianapolis, Earnhardt saw the Glen as a good place to gain points in his effort to qualify for the Chase for the NASCAR NEXTEL Cup. Although winless on the road course, he enjoys racing there and had posted finishes of third in 2003 and fifth in 2004.

[Below] Earnhardt navigates one of Watkins Glen's many turns as he tries to charge through the field after an unfortunate timing of pits stops. Starting 16th on owner points, Earnhardt suffered a setback when he pitted just before the caution came out during a series of pit stops. He restarted 37th, but the combination of a strong car and well-placed pit stops fueled a rally that paid off with a tenth-place finish.

Michigan International Speedway

GFS MARKETPLACE 400
AUGUST 21, 2005

Earnhardt leads Tony Stewart as they zip down Michigan Speedway wide and curving frontstretch. Earnhardt described this car as almost perfect at times and it showed as he ran in the top ten for all stretches. Gas mileage, however, proved to be his undoing. He had to pit with eight laps to go, a stop that doomed him to an 18th place finish. Earnhardt dropped one position to 18th as he kept his hopes alive of qualifying for the chase for the championship.

The Budweiser crew speeds through a four-tire change. Earnhardt was complimentary of his crew's efficiency but hard on himself for not getting into his pit stall properly on two occasions. Both times he pulled deep toward the front of his space to get around Greg Biffle and to give Biffle adequate room to pull out. Earnhardt's generosity resulted in having to back up before he cleared Tony Raines while leaving his pit space.

The Budweiser Chevrolet turned in one of its better intermediate track performances of the season in the GFS Marketplace 400, only to be denied a top-10 finish because of fuel mileage. Earnhardt picked his way from 16th starting position into the top 10 in the first 80 lap. He spent the next 110 laps fluctuating between seventh and 12th while engaging in three-abreast battles. A number of cars pitted near the end, and Earnhardt led one lap before he was forced to pit. The stop dropped him to 23rd and he picked up five positions in the remaining laps.

Bristol Motor Speedway

SHARPIE 500
AUGUST 27, 2005

Earnhardt hugs the bottom lane as he rumbles around one of Bristol Motor Speedway's turns banked 36 degrees. Earnhardt enjoyed an adventurous night, getting lapped by eventual winner Matt Kenseth three times and then the lucky dog award almost immediately in each incident in the first 172 laps. He escaped two wrecks with slight damage, steadily progressed over the last 250 laps of the 500-lap event and went on to a ninth-place finish.

Earnhardt romps to the inside to gain position on Jimmie Johnson, who was eventually sidelined by engine failure with 90 laps to go. Just after that, a quick pit stop under caution lifted Earnhardt into the top ten. He managed to protect his turf, even thought other drivers had fresher tires, and carved out his ninth-place finish That put him 117 points out of tenth, with two races left to qualify for the Chase for the NASCAR NEXTEL Cup by moving into the top 10.

Earnhardt waits in his pit area during the Sharpie 500 weekend. Bristol has been one of favorite tracks on the series and he had high hopes returning as the race's defending champion. He was a bit off the pace in qualifying but ground out a ninth place finish and remained mathematically in the running for a spot in the Chase for the NASCAR NEXTEL Cup.

California Speedway

SONY HD 500

SEPTEMBER 4, 2005

Earnhardt blasts through a California Speedway on three occasions, once by himself, once trailed by Dale Jarrett and once trailed by Jeff Burton. The Sony HD 500 started out on a positive note for Earnhardt as he roared from 41st starting position to into the top 20 by the 100-mile mark in the 500-mile event. The night then went quickly downhill.

Earnhardt began noticing that has engine was beginning to lose its power on the straightaways.

The problem progressively worsened as Earnhardt started losing positions, eventually dropping out of the top 30. He kept going until his engine failed in a spectacular manner as it sent rooster tails of smoke billowing from the back of the Budweiser Chevrolet. Earnhardt finished 38th and saw his chances of making the Chase for the NASCAR NEXTEL Cup come to an end as he fell 193 points out of 10th, more than the 190 points available in the only race remaining before the cutoff at Richmond.

Earnhardt sits on the pit road wall awaiting for qualifying which resulted in a disappointing 41st starting position. He came to California with hopes of remaining mathematcially elgible to gain a berth in the Chase for the NASCAR NEXTEL Cup, but that went out the window when his engine failed in a cloud of smoke.

Earnhardt talks to interim crew chief Steve Hmiel before qualifying at California. In the wake of Earnhardt failing to make the Chase for the NASCAR NEXTEL Cup, Hmiel went back to his job as Dale Earnhardt Inc.'s technical director and Tony Eury Jr. became Earnhardt's crew chief in part of the preparations for a comeback in 2006. Earnhardt and his cousin Eury were separated at the beginning of the season when Earnhardt and Michael Waltrip swapped crews. Earnhardt's record with Hmiel as crew chief included one win, three top-five finishes and five top-10 finishes in 15 races.

Richmond International Raceway
CHEVY ROCK & ROLL 400
SEPTEMBER 10, 2005

Earnhardt shoots to the outside of Jeff Gordon as they battle through a Richmond turn in the Chevrolet Rock and Roll 400. The night was not kind to either driver, but Earnhardt fared the best with his 20th place finish. Gordon stumbled to a 30th-place finish, two laps behind winner Kurt Busch and joined Earnhardt among the drivers who did not make the 10-race chase for the championship. Gordon finished the day tied with Jamie McMurray for 12th in the points. Earnhardt ended the 26-race "regular season" in 17th place.

[Above] Earnhardt zips along Richmond International Raceway's frontstrech. Earnhardt is usually among the front-runners at the .75-mile track, but he never got rolling in the Chevrolet Rock and Roll 400. After charging from 28th starting spot, he leveled off around 20th as the crew was unable to correct a tight condition which made the Budweiser Chevrolet push in the turns. The night really turned sour when Earnhardt was caught in a multi-car crash on lap 357 of the 400-lap event. He managed to stay on the lead lap and finished 20th.

[Left] Earnhardt shows a concerned look during practice. He came to Richmond seeking to rebound after his engine failure at California left him out of the Chase for the NASCAR NEXTEL Cup. He improved only slightly after the weekend as Earnhardt qualifying 28th and struggled to stay in the top 20.

Earnhardt cracks a smile as he waits for qualifying to begin. After failing to qualify for the Chase for the NASCAR NEXTEL Cup, Earnhardt and his crew began the process of building for 2006 at Richmond.

New Hampshire International Speedway
SYLVANIA 300
SEPTEMBER 18, 2005

Earnhardt looks over the Budweiser Chevrolet before the Sylavania 300, anxious to start his first race following the return of his cousin Tony Eury Jr. to the No.8 team as crew chief. The two Juniors clicked immediately as Earnhardt turned in one of his best non-restrictor plate runs of the season. He started third, stayed among the leaders all day and finished fifth. He was the only one among the top eight who was not one of those involved in the Chase for the NASCAR NEXTEL Cup.

The Budweiser crew hustles through a four-tire change. Quick pit work and pit strategy kept Earnhardt in contention all day and helped him come away with a fifth-place finish. Of five stops on the day, the fastest lasted just 12.4 seconds.

Earnhardt cuts inside Jeff Gordon heading into the first turn in New Hampshire International Speedway in a battle of drivers who were in their first race with a new crew chief after failing to qualify for the Chase for the NASCAR NEXTEL Cup championship. Earnhardt was reunited with his cousin Tony Eury Jr., reestablishing a combination dating to Earnhardt's days in the NASCAR Busch Series. Steve Letarte, an engineer, became a crew chief for the first time when he was promoted after Robbie Loomis stepped down on Gordon's team. Earnhardt got the better bump from the switches as he finished third. Gordon qualified third but faded after a strong start anD finished 14th.

Dover International Speedway

MBNA NASCAR RACEPOINTS 400

SEPTEMBER 25, 2005

Before a packed house at Dover International Speedway, the Budweiser Chevrolet crew sprints from right side to left side in the middle of changing four tires. Their most impressive work came when Dale Earnhardt Jr. came into the pits without any brakes on Lap 20. He returned to the track just seven laps down and went without trouble the rest of the day while keeping pace with the leaders.

Earnhardt drives away from Chase for the NASCAR NEXTEL Cup contender Matt Kenseth. Depsite a pit stop to correct early brake trouble, Earnhardt demonstrated he had one of the fastest cars by consistantly running with the leaders. At one point, he stayed ahead of the leader for nearly 30 laps to pick up a lap. Kenseth, who ran with the leaders much of the year, saw his day go awry when he blew a tire and crashed on lap 368 of the 404-lap event.

Earnhardt speeds to the inside of pole-sitter Ryan Newman as they barrel through one of sharply banked turns at the track known as "The Monster Mile." Newman led the first 30 laps then dropped off the pace on the way to a fifth-place finish. Earnhardt showed that he had his best car ever at Dover while holding his own with the leaders after brake trouble took him out of victory contention.

Talladega Superspeedway

UAW-FORD 500

OCTOBER 2, 2005

Earnhardt tries to shoot between pole-sitter Elliott Sadler and Jimmie Johnson. Earnhardt eventually found himself third in the outside line behind Sadler and Johnson when Sadler received a tap from Johnson. Earnhardt and Mark Martin, with little time to react, slammed into Johnson as a multi-car pileup developed. Earnhardt's DEI teammate Michael Waltrip ran over the front of Martin's car and flipped during the fracas. Waltrip, Sadler, Earnhardt. Martin and Mike Skinner were in the garage. Earnhardt wound up 40th, his next-to-worst Talladega finish.

It's a traffic jam at 190 miles an hour. Earnhardt, with Sterling Marlin in his wake, goes to the outside to get around Kasey Kahne (9), Jeff Burton (31) and Tony Stewart (20) on Talladega Superspeedway's frontstretch. Three-abreast racing is common at the mammoth 2.66-mile track, but four-abreast is unusual. However, Earnhardt was anxious to get to the front and had the power to do it as he charged from 20th starting position. The charge came to an end when he was caught in a massive wreck on lap 20 while running near the front of the pack.

Earnhardt and longtime friend Dale Jarrett chat just outside the garage building during a break in practice. A massive wreck on lap 20 kept Earnhardt from having a shot to finish either first or second as he did in a string of seven races. Jarrett, approaching the end of his career, demonstrated that he hasn't forgotten all the tricks of restrictor-plate racing. Grabbing the lead just before the caution flag was waved on the final lap, Jarrett scored his second Talladega Superspeedway victory that snapped a 13-losing streak for Ford dating to Jarrett's win in 1998.

Kansas Speedway

BANQUET 400
presented by ConAgra Foods
OCTOBER 9, 2005

Squarely in the groove. The Budweiser Chevrolet hugs the preferred line as it thunders through a turn early in the Banquet 400. The car's pristine look was ruined on lap 16 when Earnhardt collided with the slower car of Brandon Ash and then clanged against Dale Jarrett's car. The incident left the Budweiser Chevrolet with significant left side damage and uncompetitive the rest of the day. Earnhardt had to endure just trying to stay out of everybody's way over the remaining laps and was forced to settle for a 34th-place finish, two laps behind winner Mark Martin.

Earnhardt peeks inside the cockpit of the Budweiser Chevrolet, making sure everything is properly in place before he climbs aboard to compete in the Banquet 400. Earnhardt was glad everything was in order when he was involved in a crash with the slower car of Brandon Ash that did significant damage to the Budweiser Chevrolet.

Earnhardt stands beside the Budweiser Chevrolet before a packed grandstand at Kansas Speedway prior to the start of the Banquet 400. Some of the most enthusiastic fans have filled the 1.5-mile track each year since it joined the NASCAR NEXTEL Cup series in 2001.

Lowe's Motor Speedway

UAW-GM QUALITY 500

OCTOBER 15, 2005

Dale Earnhardt Jr. leads Jeff Burton through a turn during a practice session for the UAW-GM 500. Earnhardt qualified just 27th but had one of the strongest cars when the green flag fell on the 500-mile race. He needed only 27 laps to crack the top ten and was in seventh place on the 61st lap when he blew a right-front tire at the end of the frontstretch and slammed into the turn one wall. The impact badly damaged the right side of the Budweiser Chevrolet and forced Earnhardt to settle for a 42nd-place finish.

Earnhardt has a look of determination as he takes a break in practice at Lowe's Motor Speedway. Earnhardt always wants to do well on his home track, but his ambitions were derailed when he became one of nine drivers who blew tires and crashed. The tire failures were linked to heat from constant record speeds on a track made very smooth by two rounds of grinding.

Earnhardt looks like a jet-fighter pilot as he pears out of his helmet, getting ready to take the Budweiser Chevrolet out for a spin in practice. The headgear was much needed when a right-front tire blew and sent the Budweiser Chevrolet careening into the wall with a hard impact just 61 laps into the 500-mile event at Lowe's Motor Speedway.

Martinsville Speedway

SUBWAY 500

OCTOBER 23, 2005

Dale Earnhardt Jr. squeezes his way past a slower car in one of Martinsville Speedway's tight turns. He was a fixture in the top ten until getting a bumped from Kevin Harvick, spinning on the backstretch and getting brushed by Elliott Sadler just before the halfway mark in the 500-lap race. He eventually caught enough breaks to return to the lead lap but his hopes for a good finish when he ran into the rear of Travis Kvapil when Kvapil slowed going into turn one with six laps to go.

A close-up of the tire marks and scrapes on the Budweiser Chevrolet as result of the pushing and shoving common as drivers try to make passes in Martinsville Speedway's tight turns. At the end of the Subway 500, the damage was more extensive, the result of two wrecks.

Earnhardt jokes with his crew during a practice session that made a big difference. Earnhardt qualified 20th, but the changes made to the Budweiser Chevrolet during the practice runs made it one of the better cars after the Subway 500 began. He moved into the top 10 in the first 40 laps but his charge came to an end when he was spun by Kevin Harvick coming off turn two on lap 240. A wreck in the last 10 laps sent Earnhardt to a 19th-place finish.

The Budweiser crew goes through its paces while completing a routine stop of refueling and tire changing. Pit stops are critical at Martinsville because of bottlenecks that can occur on a tight pit road. Earnhardt's crew was efficient as always and helped him stay in the top 10 until a wreck put a crimp in his day.

Earnhardt tightens up his helmet before some practice laps at Martinsville.

Fans love the short track at Martinsville where they can enjoy an up close view of their favorite drivers.

Atlanta Motor Speedway

BASS PRO SHOPS MBNA 500

OCTOBER 30, 2005

Earnhardt roars down Atlanta Motor Speedway's frontstretch on the way to his strongest showing of the season. Earnhardt started 17th and 142 laps, 115 more than he had in the previous 32 races, on the way to a fourth-place finish. He went in front for the first time on Lap 53 and led at will until eventual winner Carl Edwards took command on Lap 208. Earnhardt wasn't quite as strong over the remaining 117 laps but finally showed the potential of the Budweiser Chevrolet after being derailed by wrecks for four straight weeks.

Earnhardt duels with Jeff Gordon in a battle of drivers who showed they are both turning things around preparing for 2006 with new crew chiefs and after missing the Chase for the NASCAR NEXTEL Cup championship in 2005. Gordon roared to second place a week after finishing first at Martinsville, giving much of the credit to new crew chief Steve Letarte, who replaced Robbie Loomis. Dale Jr. was virtually untouchable for a 200-mile stretch as he showed being reunited with Tony Eury Jr. is paying dividends.

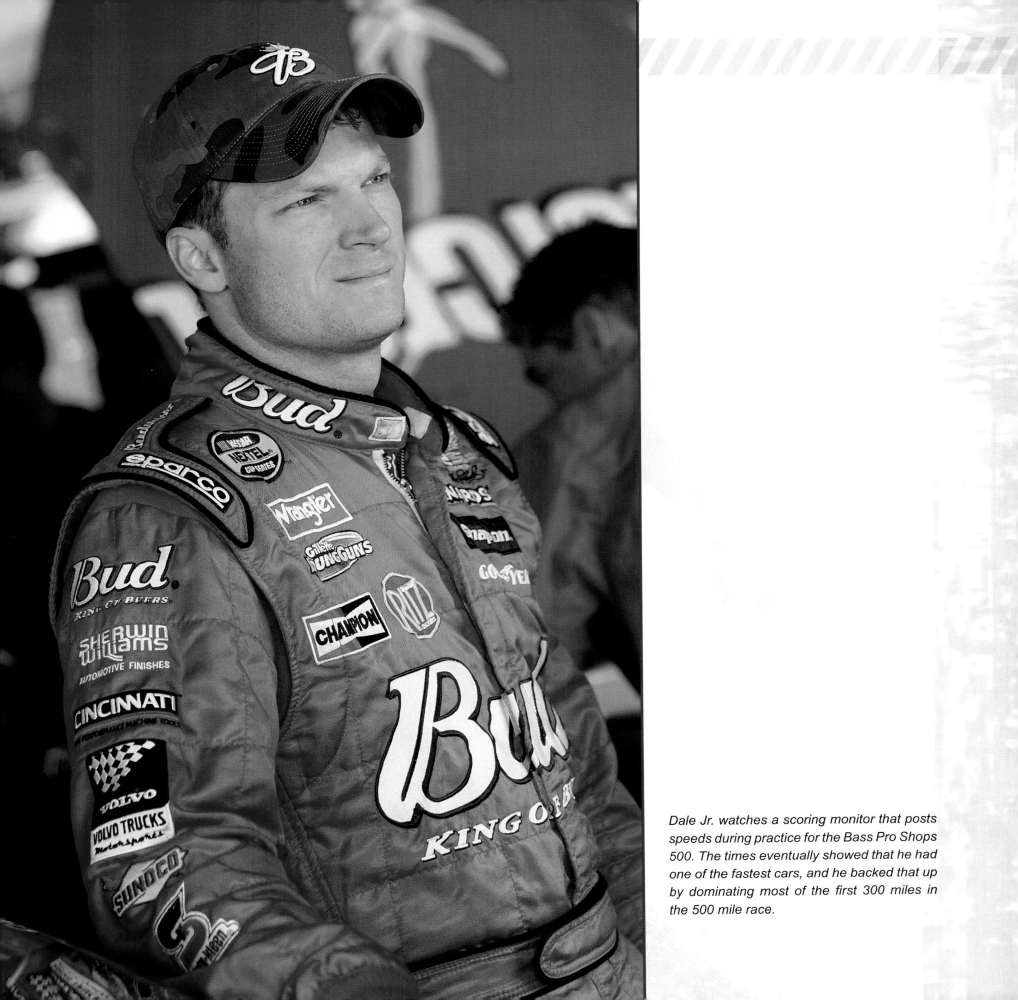

Dale Jr. watches a scoring monitor that posts speeds during practice for the Bass Pro Shops 500. The times eventually showed that he had one of the fastest cars, and he backed that up by dominating most of the first 300 miles in the 500 mile race.

A tire rolls toward crew members waiting behind the pit wall as the Budweiser Chevrolet gets a tank of fuel and four fresh tires before a full frontstretch grandstand at Atlanta Motor Speedway. The track showed few signs of damage from an F2 tornado that struck on the night of July 6 that damaged virtually every building on the property. Damage to the frontstretch suites was so bad that they had to be rebuilt.

After a strong showing and a fourth place finish, Earnhardt was quick to say a lot of the credit should be steered toward Tony Eury Jr.

Texas Motor Speedway

DICKIES 500
NOVEMBER 6, 2005

Dale Earnhardt Jr. roars down a straightaway at Texas Motor Speedway. Earnhardt qualified 10th, giving him hope of leading the most laps as he did at Atlanta Motor Speedway. He managed to stay in the top ten most of the day even though the Budweiser Chevrolet began pushing a few laps after each tire change. Earnhardt battled the whole way and finished eighth.

[Above] A bearded Elliott Sadler puts his arm around Earnhardt in a bear hug prior to qualifying for the Dickie's 500. Both drivers are past winners at Texas and saw the 500-mile race as a chance to get back into victory lane. It didn't turn out that way as they ended with respectable finishes. Earnhardt crossed the finish line eighth and Sadler finishing ninth.

[Left] Earnhardt zips along as shadow covers the frontstretch at Texas Motor Speedway in the middle stages of the Dickies 500. The race was the first at Texas to start in late afternoon and finish under the lights. Although not as fast as eventual winner Carl Edwards, Earnhardt had a top-10 car for most of the 334-lap event.

Two legends in red cars, Earnhardt sweeps inside former champion Bill Elliott as they barrell along the frontstretch at Texas Motor Speedway. Earnhardt stayed in the lead lap all day and finished eighth thanks to a decision to change two tires instead of four on a late pit stop. Elliott, who has 44 wins in his career and ran a limited schedule for Ray Evernham in 2005, finished 32nd, a lap down to winner Carl Edwards.

Taking a break in practice, Earnhardt sets sights on finishing the season strongly. After being stymied by wrecks and mechanical troubles in five straight races, he posted his second straight top-ten finish. However, the eighth place was a bit of a letdown after his strong fourth at Atlanta a week earlier. "Eighth isn't great, and the car was never as good as I really wanted, but we were able to run near the front," Earnhardt said.

Phoenix International Raceway
CHECKER AUTO PARTS 500
NOVEMBER 13, 2005

Dale Earnhardt Jr. zips along the front stretch at Phoenix International Raceway on a beautiful autumn day. After logging just the 19th fastest speed in qualifying, it was a different story for the Budweiser Chevrolet in the Checker Auto Parts 500. He charged into the top 10 and was clocking faster laps than the leader just before the caution flag waved on Lap 82. When the green flag came out again, he reported that the car was awesome. Eighth on the restart, he moved into seventh before his right-front tire went flat and sent him into the wall, ending a quest for a third straight November victory.

[Above] Earnhardt spends time on pit road before the start of the Checker Auto Parts 500. It was a weekend that he looked forward to with great anticipation, given that he was seeking a third straight November victory at Phoenix International Raceway and was coming off solid performances the previous two weeks at Atlanta and Texas. He had a fast car once again, driving quickly from a starting spot in the middle of the 43-car field. Unfortunately, bad luck struck for the fifth time in seven races as a flat tire caused a slide into the wall and a permanent trip to the garage area.

[Right] Earnhardt leads a pack of cars as he shoots in front of Rusty Wallace early in the Checker Auto Parts 500. Earnhardt started 19th, cracked the top 10 by Lap 70 and appeared to have a car capable of another top-five Phoenix finish.

[Above] The right side of the Budweiser Chevrolet was reduced to scarred and mangled sheet metal after its meeting with Phoenix International Raceway's turn three wall on Lap 113 of the Checker 500. The damage was beyond repair, dooming Earnhardt to a 40th-place finish. Notice the wall's light blue paint left down the car's side by the crash impact.

[Left] A worker for Goodyear rolls away one of Earnhardt's tires as the Budweiser crew loads the No.8 Budweiser Chevrolet into its hauler following a wreck that ended the day for the team. The outcome continued a late season pattern in which wrecks have prevented Earnhardt from displaying the full potential of a very fast car.

Homestead - Miami Speedway

FORD 400

NOVEMBER 20, 2005

Dale Earnhardt Jr. poses with his entire road crew prior to the start of the Ford 400 on a lovely day in south Florida. Earnhardt finished the season with a win, seven finishes in the top five and 13 finishes in the top 10. However, five wrecks and one engine failure put him on the sidelines six times, resulting in a disappointing 20th in final points.

Taking the high road, Earnhardt roars through turn four solidly in the top groove near the wall during the Homestead-Miami Speedway Ford 400. The 1.5 mile track's turns have progressive banking that increases from bottom to top, making it easier for drivers to run different lines. Earnhardt finished 19th, failing to have a car capable of running in the top ten for the first time in the ten races since Tony Eury Jr. took over as crew chief. Earnhardt qualified 40th for the 267 lap event. He then cracked the top 20 position mark at the Lap 150 but never got above 15th position and was lapped with just under 30 laps to go.

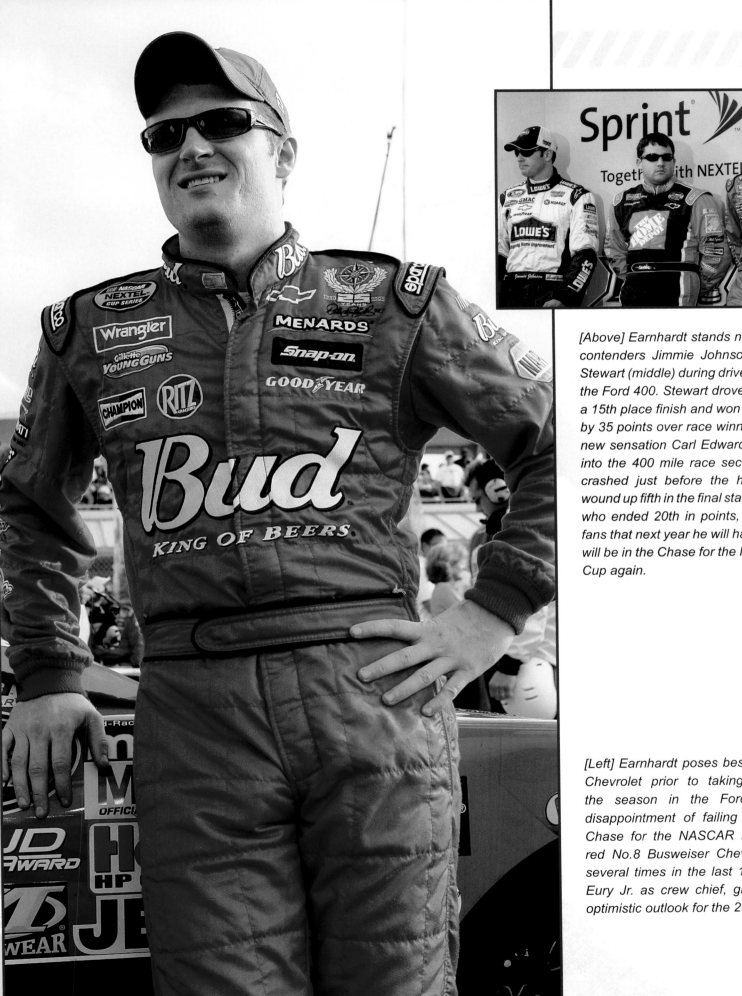

[Above] Earnhardt stands near championship contenders Jimmie Johnson (left) and Tony Stewart (middle) during driver introductions for the Ford 400. Stewart drove conservatively to a 15th place finish and won the championship by 35 points over race winner Greg Biffle and new sensation Carl Edwards. Johnson came into the 400 mile race second in points, but crashed just before the halfway mark and wound up fifth in the final standings. Earnhardt, who ended 20th in points, has vowed to his fans that next year he will have more wins and will be in the Chase for the NASCAR NEXTEL Cup again.

[Left] Earnhardt poses beside the Budweiser Chevrolet prior to taking his last ride of the season in the Ford 400. After the disappointment of failing to qualify for the Chase for the NASCAR NEXTEL Cup, the red No.8 Busweiser Chevrolet ran strongly several times in the last 10 races with Tony Eury Jr. as crew chief, giving Earnhardt an optimistic outlook for the 2006 season.

AUTOGRAPHS